THE STORY OF "CURVY KATE"

The Story of
Curvy Kate

HOWARD JAMES PIETERSIE

Copyright © Howard Pietersie, 2018

All rights reserved. Without limiting the rights under copyright reserved above, no part of this publication may be reproduced, stored in or introduced into a retrieval system, or transmitted, in any form or by any means (electronic, mechanical, photocopying, recording or otherwise), without the prior written permission of the copyright owner.

 A catalogue record for this book is available from the National Library of Australia

ISBN: 9780648172000 (paperback)
       9780648172017 (hardback)

Cover design / artwork: Laila Savolainen, Pickawoowoo Publishing Group

Interior layout: Pickawoowoo Publishing Group

Printed & Channel Distribution
Lightning Source | Ingram (USA/UK/EUROPE/AUS)

SS100 "CURVY KATE"

About the Car:

This vehicle (the only one of its kind in existence) was built in Northam, Western Australia between 2005 and 2012, by Howard Pietersie. Aesthetically, it is reasonably faithful to Sir William Lyon's magnificent pre-war Jaguar SS100 3.5 litre, having undergone subtle dimensional changes, such as being 75mm wider. The radiator cowl is lower and wider than the original. These changes accommodate the personal tastes of the builder and has resulted in "Curvy Kate" becoming the owners' version of this iconic sports car.

As this vehicle was classed as an ICV – Individually Constructed Vehicle – as opposed to a re-build, it was subjected to the Australian Design rules pertaining to new cars during its construction, resulting in some interesting challenges.

Specifications:

Body: All steel construction, hand-beaten 1mm cold rolled mild steel

Chassis: 100x50x3 RHS dimensionally similar to the original

Engine: Specially prepared 250HP straight six, fuel injected OHC, 4 litre

Gearbox: 4-speed manual

Suspension: Front – Independent double wishbone
              Rear – Live axle with trailing arms and Watts linkage

Brakes: 4 wheel discs, power assisted with dual hydraulic systems

Steering: Non power assisted rack and pinion

Contents

PREFACE ix
ACKNOWLEDGEMENTS xi

PART ONE 1
1. IN THE BEGINNING 1
2. CONTACT 5
3. THE WHEELS FALL OFF 9
4. HUNTING AND GATHERING 17
5. CONSTRUCTION BEGINS 25
6. REALITY SETS IN 31
7. THE ENGINE 37
8. GIFTS AND BAD TIDINGS 43
9. OUT OF THE BLUE & A STRANGE ENCOUNTER 47
10. A SPANNER IN THE WORKS 51
11. A CHANGE OF DIRECTION 55

PART TWO 67
12. ENGAGING GEARS 67
13. BRASS AND GLASS 73
14. MOMENTARY LAPSE OF REASON 79

15. RODNEY GETS THE WHEELS TURNING 87
16. WAR MUSEUM 95
17. ENTER THE TITANIC... 101
18. GEOMETRY REVISITED 107
19. IGNITION... 113
20. EAST EUROPEAN WIZARDRY 119

ABOUT THE AUTHOR 149

Preface

The Story of Curvy Kate covers a detailed progression of events which sometimes unfold in a reasonably normal manner, though are frequently interrupted by devastating oversights, along with many comparably comical and memorable moments.

Along the way, the author is mercilessly honest with the reader, as he stumbles through a minefield of seemingly insurmountable problems, but somehow finds solutions to them.

This work, although perceived to be a comical and satirical look at the author, also shows many occasions when the pressure of keeping the project alive in the face of other life commitments, almost brings it down.

It is easy therefore, as the story progresses, to see that the project does become something of an emotional journey.

Acknowledgements

To Gail Jennifer Pietersie

My one and only

Thank you for your unwavering support during the journey encompassed within these chapters.

Thank you for your patience with me and my wild ideas over the years.

Thank you for your unselfishness.

And thank you for your love and for giving me your life.

Howard James Pietersie

PART ONE

CHAPTER ONE

IN THE BEGINNING It was cold in Northam on the 16th of May, 2005. My Birthday. It had been good. Spoilt as usual by my family and now Gail and myself were tucked up in bed reading. Her, something with about a million pages by Dean Koontz, myself a pictorial history of British Cars (again). I was eyeballing a gorgeous little number by Michelotti for Triumph – the Italia. The body was designed to fit a standard TR3A chassis. I turned the page. It was a black and white photo of a 1937 SS Jaguar 100 – a frontal shot taken about 30 degrees to the right. Breathtaking! I stared at it for a while, then closed the book and laid it on my bedside table. For most of my adult life, I have had this ill-conceived notion that I could build a replica of a pre-war sports car. The years were slipping away. I kept backing away. Something had to be done. I drifted into a troubled sleep, haunting images of the SS sending me on my way. In the morning, I awoke before five with a resolve I had not felt before. The decision was made. I would build a replica SS100. I was excited and I was scared. And just in case I changed my mind, I woke Gail and told her the good news.

"Howie, have you been dreaming?"

I grabbed the book and showed her the photograph. "I'm going to build a car like this."

"Oh Howie, go back to sleep – you've been dreaming."

All I said was: "You better believe it."

Gee, talk about enthusiasm. It reminded me of the time I broke the news to her about the electronic ignition I had fitted to my Rover! I went to work with a spring in my step that day and set about re-arranging my machine shop so that there was a large enough area to accommodate the project. My friend Peter Mawby dropped in late that morning for a chat and a cuppa. I told him of my intentions.

"Howie, that's a #@%*^ big job," he laughed.

"Yeah, I realise that, but I believe if I do enough research, I will find a starting point. The starting point is all important here Peter – I must make a physical inroad and that will inevitably lead to something," I told him with a confidence I was far from feeling.

"Where the hell will you find a chassis and original running gear – and if you do, will you be able to license it?"

"Peter, all these questions will have to be answered in time mate, but my first stop will be York Motor Museum. There may be one there." (Wishful thinking Pietersie.)

Peter needed to keep moving as he had a busy job with Main Roads. He is a clear thinking ex-motor mechanic with a fertile brain. When he speaks, it pays to listen. He left with a friendly wave, but wearing a grin I didn't remember seeing before – it made me feel uneasy and alone.

Oh, come now – stop being a wimp. How hard could it be??????? Over the coming days I was destined to find out. I would be meeting some very clever people who would not only frighten the life out of me, but also go on to be my saviours as I soldiered on into the unknown.

That afternoon, I rang the York Motor Museum and was greeted by a friendly voice, the owner of which turned out to be the mechanic, Martin, who happened to be one of those unsung heroes of the vintage vehicle community who bury themselves in unseen workshops, tirelessly performing all manner of miracles to help keep these old cars operational. When I paid a visit to him at a later date, I saw first-hand what a splendid job he was doing.

Anyway, I went straight in, guns blazing. "Martin, do you have a SS Jaguar on display there?" There was a cackle at the other end of the line and Martin said. "Oh no mate, my boss owns the only one I know of around the traps but last I heard it was at Fremantle Museum."

When I told him of my mission, he said there were some SS bits in the workshop somewhere and offered to let me come over and have a look. After thanking him and saying I would take him up on his offer, I hung up and immediately headed for Fremantle. Action Man me! Later on, full of excitement, I drew up outside Fremantle Museum and strode inside. After paying my entry, I went in search of the SS. Nothing! Maybe I had walked past it! Surely not! I circumnavigated again – still nothing – back to reception. I was becoming exasperated.

"Excuse me," I addressed the lady at reception, "I was told you had a SS Jaguar on display here – where can I find it?" She looked up from what she was doing, gave me a broad smile and told me cheerfully: "Mr Briggs' Jaguar is presently under restoration."

Bugger!!!

"When will it be back on display?"

"I understand that it will be early in the New Year," she said. The New Year!!!! Hell it was only May!!!!

Dragging my feet, I walked slowly back to my car and set course for Northam, feeling empty and deflated. On the way home, it occurred to me that the Museum at Whiteman Park may be able to help. So I diverted and went there. Inside, I asked a gentleman who was manning reception, if they had an SS on display.

"No cob – we haven't – why is that?" he eyed me quizzically.

"I want to build a replica," I told him boldly.

"Well, I can put you in touch with someone who owns one if you like?"

Oh man!!! The pain must have drained out of my face. Bingo! Jackpot!

So, after chatting a while with John (I believe that was the man's name – a Masarati enthusiast and owner) I went away whistling happily, armed with Ian Boughton's telephone number – it was the 19th of May.

CHAPTER TWO

CONTACT Before ringing Ian Boughton, I mulled things over. Truth be known, real help is what was needed here – photographs, mountains of information, dimensions, advice on methods of construction – the list goes on.

My experience in this field amounted to the square root of zilch. Could I be cheeky enough to ask a perfect stranger to impart all this know-how to me? Moreover, what if he asks me if I had done anything like this before? What would I say? The last thing I wanted to do was to project an image of myself as being "an enthusiastic amateur", which, I thought soberly, was precisely what I was. Yours truly – Enthusiastic Amateur. But I was not going to lie! Enough of this already. I don't think he will ask me too much about my abilities anyway. I bravely dialled the number and waited...and waited. Just before ringing out, a gruff voice materialised at the other end.

"Boughton," it announced. He sounded like he had been chewing something and I glanced at my wall clock – oh crap, it was 6.30pm, what a great start – I've rung at dinner time.

"Good evening Ian," I began waveringly. "Sorry to ring at dinner time, I ah..."

"Who is it?" he cut in.

"My name is Howie Pietersie – an acquaintance of yours at Whiteman Park told me you and your son had built an SS Jaguar and he gave me your telephone number – John I think his name is."

"That is correct," Ian said. "We have built an SS – what is your interest?"

"I would like to build one myself," I told him.

"It's a bit of a challenge – what do you know about sheet metal work?"

"Just enough to be dangerous," I lied, elevating my know-how.

He laughed, then said: "Howie, why don't you get yourself one of those Panthers – they were quite nice. You'd pick up a plum for around 60K I believe."

This was going the wrong way – so I dug my heels in. "No, no Ian, they don't even look like an SS. They don't have the same character," I said firmly. "I want the real thing – or at least something that looks like the real thing."

"Well, you've got the right approach," he said. Ian became friendly and we chatted for a while longer but if he was going to offer assistance, he wasn't letting on.

Then suddenly he asked: "Where will you get the wings and rear guards? Will you make them?"

"Probably not – they're beyond me," I confessed.

"Well, there is a feller by the name of John Byfield, knocking up a set of guards for someone in the East right now – maybe you could ask him. Do you want his number?"

"Certainly do – is he good?"

"One of the best – second only to his Dad Cliff," Ian replied.

"Would you mind if I mention your name?"

"No, go ahead – let me know how you get on," he chuckled.

I thanked Ian and hung up.

With only a few hundred cars built and the survivors scattered across the globe, it occurred to me that even a 'Tinball Wizard' like John Byfield, in a backwater like Perth, would find it most unusual to be requisitioned to build one set of guards for a SS, let alone two! He had a surprise coming.

The next day I went there. It was an old wood and iron building in

Kent Street, Canning Vale. The entrance was an opening in the side of the building. I looked inside. There was a slim, silver haired man in a dust coat, with a large speckled rooster tucked under his arm, talking to another man, who was bending something up on a press brake. The silver haired party turned and saw me, placed the rooster on the ground and walked over. This man turned out to be Mr John Byfield.

Half an hour later I was on my way, having ordered a set of guards from John – he having separated me from some of my money as a deposit – and me feeling like I was really getting somewhere. Best of all, I had now immunised myself against "copping out". There was no turning back. I pulled into the nearest pub and had a celebratory drink all on my own. I was happy.

Up until now, I had still not set eyes on one of these cars – neither a replica nor the real thing. I needed a 1:18 scale model of an SS100, so I did the first thing that came into my mind – I rung around all the hobby shops/toy shops etc. – nothing! Apparently, the dies for the SS had been sold to a new company, who were going to set up production but at the time this had not yet happened. So I tried to track down a second-hand model. I had a dentist friend who collected model cars and ships called Harry Levenstein. I dropped in to see him. Inside, receptionist Julie was attending to a man in pain. She smiled when she saw me and waved me through.

"He's in the back," she said.

I walked down the passage and into the lair he used to take refuge between patients.

"Harry," I said cheerfully. "Harry Levenstein – how the hell are you." Harry's desk was littered with paperwork. "Counting your money again are you?" I love taking the mickey out of him. "I need your help."

Harry decided to bite back that day. "You're beyond my help Boof-head. I'm a dentist not a brain surgeon."

I laughed heartily at his comical retort and slapped him across the shoulder. "Have you got a model of an SS Jaguar at home?"

"No…now what are you up to?"

CHAPTER THREE

THE WHEELS FALL OFF I told Harry of my intentions, and running true to form as usual, he threw his hands in the air and exclaimed: "Good grief Howie, what next?"

Harry is a little prone to theatrics, but we still love him. I stood there grinning at him while he ranted on.

"Hell man – building a car is just...crazy. If you want something to sink your teeth into, I know a fellow in Townsville who has a lovely old Riley just begging for life. I can approach him for you. It would be so much easier than building something – especially an SS!" He stopped to take a breath and I jumped in. Excitable boy, our Harry!

"Harry, don't jump off your horse – just listen to me. I've done my dash with restos. This will be a real challenge. Now help me you old sod. I need a model. You have connections around the country. And for that matter, headlights too. How about that mate of yours in Johannesburg. Willy somebody? He makes parts for old cars doesn't he?"

Harry is a South African Jew, from a place called Sandton, near Johannesburg, and knows lots of people in the vintage car community. He is a bit of a father figure to me and I couldn't blame him for wanting to put the brakes on me, because I do have a habit of getting ahead of myself, as readers will discover when we get further into the story. Harry secretly likes this kind of thing, but would never admit it. Anyway, he turned around and went back to his desk, shaking his head and muttering.

"Well?" I looked at him expectantly.

"Alright, alright. I'll see what I can find out, but I warn you, I'm busy at this point in time so don't pester me – these things take time!" I could see he wanted me to go. I went over and kissed him on top of the head and he pushed me away. "Get away from me now," He pulled a wry face and I shot through.

I have three friends who live in metropolitan Perth. These guys often do a brekky run on their motorcycles, to Toodyay and through to York via Northam. Sometimes they stop and I join them through to York on my little Suzuki – a 1966 T20 'Super Six' – this little jewel (a six speed 250cc two stroke twin) played a major role in toppling the British and European manufacturers. It is capable of seeing a Bonneville off, up to 80mph, and was the first production 250cc to reach the magic 'ton'. Enough of that now! Sorry...I tend to waffle on a bit about my first love – motorcycles. So back to the business at hand.

One weekend we invited the boys to have brekky at our place instead of York. The guys turned up around 9.30am, and after exchanging greetings all round, we sat down and began chatting while Gail went to the kitchen.

Bob is employed by Vehicle Licensing in the technical section at Welshpool. Fred is an inspector at the Warwick branch, and to this day I have no idea what Colin does for a crust. All top blokes. All very knowledgeable. You'll notice I tend to hang around with these talented people. Can you guess why?

First, we brought each other up to date on the latest developments in our lives. Bob had recently done a run to Albany and back on an old DT175. Fred had come a cropper on a Postie bike and Colin had just purchased an Indian Royal Enfield Bullet.

"And you Howie – what have you been up to?" Fred asked.

"Oh, mostly the same old thing but I'm looking at a new project," I informed him.

Bob chimed in: "Another project – you only finished the Rover last year!"

"Yeah, I know, but you guys know what I'm like – I get ants in my pants!"

"What's it going to be this time?" Fred asked.

"I'm thinking of doing an SS100."

"They are very hard to find," Bob commented, then continued. "I think you'll find most of them in this country are already done up!"

"No. I want to actually build one from scratch. You know – a replica!"

"A replica!" This was Bob. He seemed to draw in most of the air around us and whistled inwards. "What a great idea – but what about the chassis and running gear? All that kind of thing?"

"I doubt I'd find a chassis," I replied. "I'll just have to make a chassis as per the original."

"Hang on Howie, there are rules. Be careful here. I will tell you what you are allowed to do." Bob eyeballed me critically now, while the other two looked on intently. "If you can find a chassis and running gear, the job can be done as a restoration – which it would be. Are you with me?"

I nodded. "Go on." This was going the wrong way.

"Then as long as you use the original running gear etc., you won't have a problem," he concluded.

"What's the alternative Bob? You and I both know that it would take years to find gear like that."

"Now, you can build the car in its entirety, chassis and all, if you stick to the rules. And the rules are: First of all the engine would have to conform to the current ADRs."

I stopped him. This is definitely not what I wanted to hear. "How about, say, a 1985 Series 3 Jag engine?"

"Too old. It won't pass emission tests." Bob could see the look on my face. "Sorry mate – but you need to know. I'll send you some literature that will explain everything."

"Okay, ta."

"Basically, what the procedure is, is that first you register the project with Technical as "an Individually Constructed Vehicle", informing them of your intentions and stating what power plant etc. will be used. They will then give you permission to proceed. Then it will have to be checked by an engineer throughout the life of the build and then signed off by him. After that, it can go for inspection."

I was feeling hollow. He could see that. "Look Howie, it may not be an SS if you do it that way, but remember, as long as it looks like one and you have modern running gear, you will have a car that behaves a sight better than the original," Bob consoled soothingly.

"Yeah, I suppose," I responded, seeing some merit in this but feeling far from happy. I tried another angle in desperation – as if Bob alone could somehow wave a wand and change the rules. "How about if I put an XJ6 engine on gas – would that conform?"

Bob lifted a finger. "Ah, yes…and no. You can put it on gas, but then unfortunately, another problem arises."

"Oh, what's that?" I asked.

"It will have to be tested for emissions…"

I interrupted him. "Well, that's not too bad. Where is that done? Do you guys do that?"

"No, no, no mate – the engine will have to go to Orbital Engineering in Balcatta and apparently the price is prohibitive."

Oh crap – thank goodness I hadn't started before speaking to these guys. I decided not to tell them that I'd already placed a $300 deposit on a series 3 Jaguar.

Bob and Fred encouraged me to go ahead with the replica and reiterated the silver lining. But I failed to see it. Long after they had left, I just sat in the games room staring blankly into space. After dinner that evening, I rang Ian Boughton. "Hi Ian. It's Howie – I need to cry on your shoulder."

"What's the matter cobber – have you seen Byfield yet?"

"Yes as a matter of fact, I have – I ordered the wings and paid a deposit. But other problems have come up." I told him about the discussion with Bob. I told him I was feeling so deflated about things, that I was seriously considering pulling out. But Ian was most encouraging and, like Bob, mentioned the virtues of having a car with modern running gear. He also pointed out that the car he and Brett had restored was made up of parts that had been acquired from all over the world, and that the bits were becoming so scarce that he believed it would take me a dozen years to find everything I needed. I can't describe how much better I felt after speaking to Ian. My mood was much more buoyant, and before signing off Ian expressed his approval of me having got the wings ordered and told me not to hesitate to call him should I need any other advice. He also gave me Brett's telephone number with the intention of arranging a meeting to have a look at their car. I couldn't wait to come face to face with 'Miss SS110'.

Northam is a town of around 7000 people situated in a valley about 75km from Midland, which is at the eastern extremity of metropolitan Perth. The locals enjoy freezing cold winters and blistering hot summers. But we survive. My workshop is a 150 square metre affair, sandwiched between three others, slap in the middle of the town's industrial area. It's nothing to get excited about, but it suits me and the rent is reasonable.

One morning as I drove through the gates and headed down the drive to my factory unit, I saw a car was parked outside the roller door. A man was padding up and down near the car, chatting into a mobile phone. It turned out to be Peter Mawby. Waving a greeting to him as I climbed out of Gail's Mini (which I had decided to use that day), I went about my usual morning ritual. First, the side door, then the roller door, followed by the lights, the kettle and finally, the radio. Peter spoke on the phone for some time, while I got myself ready for work. I spared a minute to inspect the vehicle he had turned up in. It was an early two-door Volvo 140 series, powder blue in colour and in great condition for its age. Peter finished on the phone and joined me now.

"Good Morning Howie," he said cheerfully.

"Morning Peter," I jabbed a thumb over my shoulder at the car. "Who belongs to that little beauty?" I enquired.

"It's my father's car Howie. He purchased it new, back in 1973."

"Gee, she's in good shape. What's the go – why did you bring her today? Something gone wrong with the old Honda?" I asked.

"No, no – it's the Volvo. I believe there is a worn ball joint under there somewhere. I wondered if I could jack her up later today in your shop and have a look?"

"Yes, certainly mate. Go for your life – anytime," I told him.

After that, Peter shot through and I got started as well. The idea of building this car was becoming all consuming, and I was finding it increasingly difficult to detach myself from the project and concentrate on my work. At the time I was building a press tool for punching out the clamps that hold temporary fencing together. It was for a scaffolding company. I forced all thoughts of exotic sports cars from my mind and got on with it. By the time Peter turned up that afternoon, I was quite pleased with my progress. It was 4pm and I could make out a quiet whimpering emanating from the fridge. It was the beer calling. I ripped the top off a Cascade Light and inhaled it while I sat waiting for Peter. It wasn't long before he turned up. He pulled the Volvo in immediately and got out.

"Good afternoon Howie."

"Hi Peter – go ahead," I told him. "Sing out if you need anything. I'll be working on my bike."

"Okay, ta."

I went over to the stand where I had been servicing my motocross bike and began tinkering with the air filter while Pete donned a pair of overalls. It was strange to see him in overalls as he normally dressed in smart civies every day. He jacked up the front of the Volvo and slid underneath. I was feeling playful, so I gave him a rev.

"If you need any expert advice, just call out."

"Yeah, Yeah."

Five minutes later he was under the car with a crowbar, testing for wear. Much grunting noises, followed by a loud snapping sound from under the car, followed by unprintable curses. I called out to him as I rushed over to see what had happened.

"Are you alright Pete? What happened?" I asked anxiously, quickly sliding under the car beside him. He was lying on his back, arms outstretched, with the crowbar lying on his chest. I could see he was okay, but a knob was already forming on his forehead. It looked funny – so I laughed. I couldn't help it.

"Callous bastard," he murmured and then smiled. "What do you think fucking happened?" I smiled too, then we both began laughing aloud.

Full of surprises, my mate Pete. Talk about changing the subject. "Have you forgotten that cockeyed idea of yours about building the car yet?"

"No."

"Well, Howie, if you're really serious, have a look around under here." I obeyed.

Above me was an exquisite looking cross-member with unequal 'A' arms and lovely long steering arms, and at each end, nice chunky componentry with large diameter discs and twin pod callipers. "Gee Pete, this is good gear for an old car – four wheel discs and all," I commented, impressed.

"And the brakes are fully twin system. They work well," he added.

"What about down the back," I asked craning my neck. There was a live axle with trailing arms and a Watts linkage.

"What do you think?" Pete asked.

I lay there for a moment before answering. Here in front of me was the perfect setup for my project – uncluttered, well proven – everything I needed. And these cars were easy to find!

"What do I think? Pete, what I think is that it was a great idea that you brought this car here today. A great idea." My mind was racing. Now I just wanted to get started. I needed to contact Brett Boughton.

"Oh yeah, did you find the problem?" I asked Pete. I'd forgotten all about it. And his head too!

"Yes, it's the upper right ball joint – easy fix."

"Well, let's go put some ice around your nut," I told him.

We got out from under the car and returned to my kitchen to sort his head out, but he waved me away.

"It's okay." Pete headed for the kettle and made himself a brew before heading back to Perth.

I closed up and went away feeling like I needed to start pressing buttons and pulling levers.

CHAPTER FOUR

HUNTING AND GATHERING That evening I rang Brett Boughton. Brett turned out to be a friendly, helpful person and we chatted for a good half hour, having discussed my intentions, his car, motorcycles and many other things. By the time I rang off, it felt like I had known him for years.

His father, apparently, had filled him in earlier on my conversations with him, and Brett too assured me he would offer advice anytime. And in addition, he was preparing some 'mud maps' for me. These so called mud maps turned out to be photocopies of the original chassis, drawings painstakingly put together by them during their build, and a list of names of people around the county I could call on for parts if need be. What a legend you are Brett! I was ecstatic. Arrangements were made for us to meet at his house in Canning Vale in a couple of days to view his car. Only two more sleeps!

Later on that evening, I dug out an old Quokka from the magazine rack and frantically tracked down the appropriate page in car parts. Almost immediately my eyes fell upon an advert for Volvo parts. It was a Mundaring number – ripper. What a stroke of luck. Close to home. I glanced at the wall clock. It was 9.15pm. Too late? Probably, but to hell with it. Tough titty. I rang.

"Phil speaking." He must have been sitting next to the phone.

"Hi Phil. My name is Howie. I'm ringing about your advert for Volvo parts!" I told him expectantly.

"Yes mate. What parts are you looking for?" he asked.

"I'm chasing cross-member and all the bits. Also rear end, diff, brakes etc."

"Oh. I've plenty of that gear. Where are you ringing from?"

"Northam."

"Not too far – maybe you should come look," he suggested.

"I need to travel into Welshpool tomorrow," I told him. "What are your movements Phil?"

"I'm nearly always here, so you can front up anytime." He told me, then proceeded to give me directions on how to reach his pad from Great Eastern Highway.

"I'll see ya tomorrow – thanks Phil," I said and hung up.

What a great day it had been. Recently, for various reasons, my mood had been rising and falling as fast as the temperature in a pasteurising machine, but now I felt settled and focused on the job ahead.

I went to bed and cuddled up to Gail. "Thank you for allowing me to do this thing with the car my Baby. I love you lots." She was half asleep and simply squeezed my hand and grunted. But I knew what it meant.

Phil had told me to turn right at Mundaring lights. I followed his directions and after much twisting and turning, the road petered out deep in bushland. It was a circular cul-de-sac. Two driveways led off it and snaked their way through tall eucalypts and low scrubland.

At the entrance to one of the driveways stood a sign on a star picket, indicating the number Phil had given me. So I did what sounded like a good idea at the time – I followed it. No flies on me! Around two hundred metres down the track, the bush began to thin out. The roof of a house loomed up and the track emptied out into a clearing about an acre in size. A relatively new single-storey brick house stood smack in the middle. No gardens – well, no botanical gardens that is. Mechanical gardens, yes. That is where I found myself. Everywhere I looked, in every direction, were Volvos in various stages of decay. I'm in the right place, I mused.

Stopping my vehicle some 30 metres from the house, I climbed out and stretched my legs. Nobody around. Eerie. Also dead silence. It was late morning – not even the chirping of birds. I approached the house. The front door was closed, including the flyscreen. A red Volvo was parked close to the house. This one looked operational. Maybe this was Phil's car. To the right of the house – a carport. I should have simply rapped on the door, but I didn't. I decided to walk around. Inside the carport on blocks was yet another Volvo, but this one, a rare breed. Late sixties 122s. This was obviously in the process of restoration, though I couldn't be sure. It looked abandoned – covered in dust and cobwebs. Could be a nice collector's item I remember thinking as I made my way around the car and began walking down the side of the house, hoping to find someone.

Suddenly, at the far corner, a small dog appeared, saw me, and began to bark furiously, simultaneously belting towards me at a fair click. It was only a small creature, so I stopped and waited to see if the racket had alerted someone – if indeed, there was anyone around. He had said to come anytime, so I guessed meant he would be there all day. The little dog kept coming and I readied myself to kick it in the chops if it persisted and tried to bite me.

But then, to my horror, another dog appeared. Sliding round the corner, kicking up dust, it was in hot pursuit of the little one. But this was a big dog. It looked like a Rottweiler-cross but I wasn't hanging around to find out. Terrified, I turned and ran at top speed for the ute. Looking back as I ran, I saw the dogs were gaining on me at an alarming rate. My mind was going gangbusters! Too late even to open a door and gain refuge inside the cab.

Jump up on the tray – quick. Shit! They're on me! Up on the tray just in time. The big dog jumped up and began attempting to follow me and I clambered onto the roof of the cab, and sat facing the dog, ready to fight it off with the advantage of height. Then a voice overpowered the din and suddenly a man in overalls appeared and was shouting at the dogs, ordering them to back off. They did.

"Sorry – I forgot to warn you – but they won't bite."

"I'm not a clairvoyant," I said. "They frightened the hell out of me!"

"I'll lock them in the house," the man said, looking uncomfortable.

"What a splendid idea!" I replied and climbed down off the ute, trying to regain my composure. I was still shaken when he returned.

"Are you Phil?"

"Yes, sorry about that – I really am. Come around to the back…you must be Howie!" He ventured.

"That's me. Hunting for parts can be a dangerous pastime," I added soberly, following him.

Around the back, car parts lay everywhere. Phil seemed to know his stuff and made a list of the parts I would need, which included front end complete with brakes etc., rear end and the complete braking circuit. I asked Phil to remove all the brake pipes so that the entire circuit could be laid out on the floor to enable me to reproduce it accurately. He threw in the steering system as well as an M45 gearbox from a 264 Volvo. This unit, he claimed, was the strongest in the range. Phil came up with a figure of $500, making sure I understood that this was a very good price.

I nodded and said: "Phil, no need to convince me mate – the price is not as important as the condition of the stuff you supply me."

"It'll be very good," he assured me. "Now, you mentioned you were in Northam?"

"Yep."

"Well, in a few days' time I'm picking up a car near York. Do you want me to drop the stuff off with you?"

"That would be just spot on Phil – I'll pay something towards your fuel."

But Phil said he would do it for nothing on account of the dog attack. We both laughed and with that, after exchanging mobile numbers, I headed off to Welshpool to look after my business for the day. My workshop was running low on consumables and I had a couple of calls to make. When I'd finished, it occurred to me Brett Boughton's place wasn't far away. I wondered if he was home. Why, I couldn't tell you, for it was a work day. I called. He answered immediately.

"Hi Brett – I'm in the area and had a hunch you may be available!"

"You jagged me mate – I'm here until 3 o'clock – do you want to come across for a cuppa?"

"For sure. How do I get there?"

Brett explained and I changed course and headed for Canning Vale.

Deep in the heart of suburban Canning Vale, the road I was following became the inevitable cul-de-sac surrounded by some pretty smart looking houses. I found Brett's place amongst them, and pulled up about 10 metres from the mouth of a double garage. Brett was already standing outside facing me as I got out of the car. He must have heard the ute turn up.

I have always had a habit of surveying the geography of my surroundings when I visit a place for the first time. But after that first visit to Brett's I could not have told you what the house looked like. He'd already taken the cover off.

It was white. There were curves. There was chrome – lots of chrome. Wire wheels. Louvres. My jaw dropped and I stood and stared. Oh hell! I'd forgotten about Brett. Good heavens – I had walked straight past him! I turned quickly and grinned sheepishly.

"Sorry mate – I forgot my manners when I saw the car. She's beautiful!"

He waved the apology away and gestured to the car. "Go for your life," he prompted. "Or do you fancy a cuppa first?" He added. "Did you bring your camera and measuring tape?"

"I must confess I'm guilty as charged! I always have these things in the car as I use them for work as well."

"Good!"

Can the coffee wait until I've settled down?"

"Ha! Ha!" Brett found this amusing. "I'll go put the kettle on while you look around."

Out of the corner of my eye, I saw Brett vanish through a hole in the wall. While he was away, I took stock of things. So this is what an SS looks like in the flesh. Coming face to face with this car really meant so much to me at that moment. I must say to all you kind souls out there adventurous enough to hear my story, that the first thing that struck me when I walked around Brett's car, was its sheer presence – poise, if you will. "Just look at me!" it screamed. And the curves. One radius blending into the next. The great one must have been on a creative high to say the least when he dreamed up this masterpiece. Bless your soul Sir William.

By the time Brett returned with coffee I had settled down and retrieved my camera from the ute. He prompted: "Go ahead Howie." So I did.

For the next 10 minutes I took photos from every possible angle, of every possible component I could focus on. While this was going on, Brett pointed out the importance of getting the shape of the chassis right, because the wings were being made on their jigs and if I got that wrong, the guard wouldn't fit. Great!

"Also," he continued, "the shape of the baseline on the scuttle needs to be identical to this car."

I had got to my feet now after taking snaps under the car. "What's the scuttle Brett? Is it this part here?" I indicated to the side of the car immediately behind the bonnet.

"Yes mate – but it also includes the top, around the eyelids and under the doors!" he pointed out.

"Excuse my ignorance Brett," I said, feeling a bit silly, but continued, "so, what is this section called?" I asked pointing to the rear of the car. What would Brett be thinking? Here I was, 'Mr Clever', who was about to begin building one of these masterpieces and had no idea what I was looking at.

"No Howie – don't worry mate. The rear end is the 'Tub'…look, starting at the rear we have 'the Tub', then 'the Scuttle'," he indicated with a sweep of his hand. "Then as you know, 'the Firewall', 'Bonnet' and finally down here," he indicated to the front section below the grill, "'the Apron'."

Brett stood smiling at me as excitement began to turn to fear. The complex geometry in this bodywork was beginning to frighten the life out of me. The more I looked at it, the more worried I got. Brett could see it.

"Don't panic mate," he said. "You'll do it!"

I just shook my head and followed him into the house.

Inside, Brett said, "I've got something for you," as he pointed at the dining table. "Take a seat." Brett walked down the passage to one of the rooms.

There were two long-haired cats sitting on the couch, eyeballing me. I walked over and began stroking them. I like cats. In the right hands, they make wonderful companions. These two looked much loved.

"Nice cats," I commented when Brett returned with paperwork.

"My partner loves them," he returned.

"These are for you." He proceeded to produce a collection of drawings he and Ian had made up while they were building the white one. This paperwork would prove invaluable to me in the coming years. There was even a copy of the original chassis from Coventry.

"Really, I can't stress how much I appreciate this Brett," I said before adding "but, to be honest mate, after seeing your car, I've realised that I'm in over my head – scared actually."

"Don't be – you're a toolmaker, you'll work it out. I know you will – just treat each part of the job as a project on its own – don't think about the car, because that will get you into trouble."

"Alright Brett. You're probably right – I need to get started on the job asap. Look, thanks for all your help mate, I need to keep moving now. Good to meet you." We shook hands.

"Ditto mate – keep us informed."

"I certainly will." With that I headed for home.

But before I did, I enquired: "What do you do for a crust, if you don't mind me asking".

"I teach science Howie," he answered.

"Oh, Wow!"

"No big deal mate. No big deal. I, like you, served an engineering apprenticeship."

"Toolmaker as well?" I enquired.

"No. Mine was a little bit different. My handle is 'Scientific Instrument Maker'. Very interesting stuff. I was lucky. Not just anybody can get in. You have to go into a pool, then if you get selected, you get an apprenticeship."

"You must have been good at school," I ventured.

"I struggled through," he answered with a shrug.

"I think you're a very modest person Brett." And with that, I walked over to my car and drove away.

On the way, the phone rang. "Hey Boofhead." It was Harry. "When are you coming to fetch your model?" The old fart had come through, just like I knew he would.

CHAPTER FIVE

CONSTRUCTION BEGINS Apparently, one of Harry's cronies – colleagues that is – had sold a number of Burago 1:18 scale models to a chap in Canberra. One of them had been an SS. A silver 1937.

Prompted by my mate Harry, he contacted the guy and managed to buy it back. So, the car was sent back to Hobart and then on to Perth, where it finished up in Harry's lair. It was perched on his desk when I turned up.

As soon as he saw me, he acted out his normal ritual – dropped what he was doing, leant backwards in his chair, hands behind the head – here we go!

He looked critically at me and pointed to the silver SS on the desk and said "There you go. So how much is it worth to you Boofhead?"

I played along a bit. "C'mon Harry, don't start," I said laughingly. "They cost about $70 new, and this one's second-hand. And where's the box? There's no flipping box!"

"Never mind all that my friend. Supply and demand is the issue here – and my time doesn't come cheap either." (Don't remind me I thought.)

"You old prick. How much? C'mon!"

Indicating that the joke was now over, Harry got serious. "The cheeky sod in Canberra had it on his mantle collecting dust. He wanted $150."

"Bloody robber," I agreed, but then picked up the model and quickly slipped around the desk and kissed him on top of his bald nut. "I love you Harry."

He pushed me away roughly. "Stop that – now take your car and go – go on!"

"I'm going. I'm going – I'll bring whiskey!" So I went. But not before sticking my head back around the wall from the passage and giving him another rev. "How did you go with those headlights, by the way?"

This time he glared at me and drew breath noisily, but before he had time to shout obscenities, I shot through, cackling to myself as I went. The secretary was looking down at her keyboard, silently quaking and shaking her head.

When I got to my car, I realised I had forgotten to pay him. Never mind, I would fix him up when I brought the bottle.

It was Friday afternoon, and I drove home thoughtfully, the little car perched on the dash in front of me, so I could eyeball it on the way. I was like an excited school boy. I simply could not wait to get started. But I should really hang in there for the Volvo bits first. The chassis would need to be designed around the dimensions of the front cross-member. Or at least, that was the way I saw it.

That entire weekend I buried myself in paperwork. The drawings Brett had given me were invaluable while I studied the accuracy of the Burago model. I was able to extract a host of critical dimensions from the sketches that enabled me to compare them to the scaled-up dimensions of the model. I compared the many photos of Brett's car to the model and found it to be extremely well proportioned. Almost every dimension I scaled up closely matched Brett's drawings. This was of paramount importance as its accuracy would allow me to calculate sizes and angles etc, that were missing. So, armed with photos, sketches and the little silver SS, I prepared myself to venture bravely into the engineering project of my life.

Now, turning the clock back about two years, I was polishing my newly restored Rover V8 in the workshop one day (when I was meant to be working), when a slim, sharp featured individual appeared in the mouth of the roller door. I put the polish rag on the roof of the Rover and walked over to him.

"G'day. Can I help?"

The man stepped forward and offered his hand. "I'm Frank," he announced.

"Howie," I reciprocated, and Frank continued "How do you do – perhaps you can help me with a project. I need some machining work done for a military vehicle I'm building."

"Gee – that sounds interesting – a military vehicle hey. What kind of military vehicle?" I asked, quickly becoming curious as this was my kind of language.

"Well Howie, I recently picked up a World War II British armoured car – or what was left of it. The idea is to cut it back and convert it to the German equivalent," Frank explained.

"Wow, sounds like work to me – shitloads of it," I observed.

"True, true," Frank agreed, "but it's what makes my world go around."

"Mine too! So, let's have a look at what you're chasing," I said to him with a grin, and he produced a collection of sketches. We walked over to the corner of the workshop I call the office (open plan). Frank spread his paperwork across the desk.

"I need shafts, bushes, housings, pins and so on for the drivetrain. Also, replicas of the guns. They don't need to be identical, but they do need to look the part."

"That shouldn't be a problem Frank!"

"So, are you interested in doing the job Howie?" he asked expectantly.

"Sure mate. Sure. But if you don't mind me asking, why a German armoured car – why not a British one? I would have thought it easier to reproduce what was already there." People with enquiring minds often come across as being nosy. I hoped Frank didn't think I was being nosy now.

"Ah, no worries. I collect German war memorabilia. Vehicles, books, medals, uniforms – actually anything and everything related to the German war effort," he explained.

"Well, I'll be damned. What a magic hobby."

Anyway, after yakking for a while about warplanes and the like, we went through Frank's requirements. I knocked up some quick sketches of the various components and worked out a rough production schedule, so as to fit in with his projected progress. After that, Frank thanked me and said he would keep in touch. We then exchanged mobile numbers and he departed, perched on top of a rather tired looking early model Yamaha trail bike.

So, by now, understandably, the reader would begin to ask the question: "What has all this to do with an SS Jaguar?" Well, the author begs forgiveness for drifting away from the subject, but on that seemingly ordinary business day eight years ago, there was no way to tell that this interesting and obviously intelligent man would finish up playing a vital role in the creation of 'Curvy Kate', who herself (at that time) was not even a twinkle in the eye of the creator. Not ten minutes after Frank had left, Jack, the guy in the adjoining factory unit, breezed in to ask my advice about an alternator he was tinkering with.

"I see Frank from Valley Ford paid you a visit," he commented sociably.

"Yeah. He wants some machining done," I returned, without elaborating on the details, in case Frank was keeping his project under wraps. People do these things for a variety of reasons, I've found.

"Clever boy – our Frank. Clever boy," Jack said, then added, "what he's probably forgotten about Fords, other people still have to learn. Top technician."

True to his word, Phil rang me during the following week and arranged to drop the parts off. Prior to that, I had arranged for Midalia Steel to deliver a couple of lengths of RHS tubing, for the chassis. During the weekend I had designed the chassis longitudinal members, so was ready to get started on cutting and bending the material. I had cleared part of the wall behind where the car would begin to take shape, and pinned up all the informative literature, drawings and photographs I possessed. Two chunky trestles stood waiting. My drop saw was positioned not too far away from the site. All this was set up directly across the way from my lathe, milling machine and surface grinder so I could eyeball everything at a glance – even when I was working.

The little model was perched atop a shelf above the board carrying all the technical information. I walked fearlessly over to the first length of material – 100x50x30 RHS, which was already set up in my saw. I donned my safety glasses and activated the trigger. The drop saw screamed in anger and tore through the RHS, producing the very first part of my dream.

It was 2.35pm.

The date: The Twenty First of July, 2005.

CHAPTER SIX

REALITY SETS IN As expected, Phil, en route to York to pick up the car, presented himself at my factory unit, my bits spread out in his car trailer.

With a practiced hand, he manoeuvred it into a position so as to reverse up to the wall alongside the roller door. Using the customary hand signals, I indicated for him to start coming.

I have this uncanny ability to attract problems. When the trailer was about a metre from the wall, I raised my hand, signaling for him to stop. He kept coming. Wait for it! Then I was waving my arms like Kaiser Bill's batman and yelling out, but to no avail. Phil couldn't be watching me, I realised at the last second. It all happened so quickly. I watched helplessly as the trailer rammed the Zincalume wall, leaving a sizeable dent and demolishing the taillights. What the blazes was he thinking? The silly sod. Or what wasn't he?

"What were you thinking mate?" I blurted out as he stumbled out of the car and came and stood beside me.

"I don't know. I just don't know!" he stammered.

"Didn't you see my signals?"

"No, I wasn't looking – sorry, I'm used to doing these things on my own."

"Really?" I grinned at him, now realising the poor sod was feeling genuinely embarrassed by the incident.

"Oh shit. I'm terribly sorry!" said Phil, looking dejected.

I laid a hand on his shoulder "Not such a good start to the day, eh mate?"

Phil offered to pay for the damage. I waved the suggestion away.

"Nah! It's only a dent! I'll sort it out. Now, let's have a gander at what you've got for me."

Back in Mundaring on the day Phil's dogs had tried to make a meal of me, I had impressed upon him that I needed the entire braking system. It could be laid out on the floor of the workshop. I would take notes and photos so that the circuit could be rebuilt as per factory when the time came. Phil was great. Once we had offloaded, he laid out all the components in position on the floor, including brakes and steering. It was all filthy but at the price of $500 I hardly expected it all to be clean. It didn't matter. All would be reconditioned anyway.

After Phil had left, I spent some time taking some sizes and snaps, then just stood there for a while studying the general layout.

Geez! Just cleaning this stuff up is going to be a project in itself, I remember thinking soberly. The immensity of what I was taking on had not yet fully registered, but the now familiar fluttering in my stomach began again.

Later that day, sometime after lunch, I was leaning on the corner of the bench next to my lathe while a cut was in progress through the bore of a wet sleeve. I was working on some artefact of the past for a member of the local Antique Machinery Club.

While this was going on, I was gazing thoughtfully at the mechanical skeleton laid out on the floor. In particular, the steering box and associated linkages etc. Something was bothering me about this. There was something sinister lurking here. I couldn't put my finger on it, so I left it and carried on with my job. But from time to time as the afternoon wore on towards 'beer time', it kept coming back to niggle me. Now, had my name been Ian Boughton, I'd have seen it immediately. I cracked open a beer – as if that would somehow help – and pulled up a chair. Alas, no amount of eyeballing the collection of components from various angles would unlock the dark secret lurking there! The answer would come – I knew it would. I would just have to wait.

At ten past four the following morning, after the inevitable trip to the toilet, I sat on the side of the bed, listening to some kookaburras in the tree outside, and looked down at Gail gently snoring all the while thinking about that blasted steering unit. I couldn't get back to sleep. Suddenly, just before 5 o'clock, the 'gremlin' presented itself in sharp focus.

GOOD GRIEF! I WAS IN TROUBLE.

Gail was still sleeping soundly. I left the bed quietly, and hurriedly donning a tracksuit, hightailed it downstairs. It was freezing cold but I hardly noticed as I coaxed my Rover into life and headed to the workshop, without an ounce of compassion for the beautiful ice cold aluminium V8 engine thumping its disapproval along the way. On the desk were two workshop manuals. I snatched one up and tracked down the section covering the steering box. On the Volvo, the steering box is mounted on the inside of the chasses rail, and the arm faces forward, as the steering arms are at the front. I then went over to the cross-member on the floor and offered up a piece of 100x50 RHS to the top of the mounting point and clamped it in position to mimic a chassis rail. I held the steering box up to the rail, as close as possible to the position dictated by the picture in the manual. Then my worst fears were realised. As the location of the steering box is dictated by the relative positions of the linkages leading to the steering arms, it became apparent that the mounting position was fixed.

All you talented types out there, kind enough to hear my story, would no doubt have asked some intelligent questions about the system intending to be used, rather than diving in head first like yours truly – Mr Ironstein – I'm sure! And so, you, after careful consideration and after studying the geometry of the SS Jaguar bodywork and the Volvo mechanics, would have deduced that the steering box was going to present itself in full view above the louvered apron of the SS, half buried by the radiator cowl!

I went home then. Shattered. There was no way out of this, short of changing the very fundamentals of my plan, which would have meant discarding the Volvo front end. And then there would be a chain reaction.

Gail was in the family room, sipping coffee. "Where did you go?" she asked sleepily.

"To the workshop."

"What for, for heaven's sake? You could have told me!"

"I'm sorry. I'm in major strife with the project!"

"Why, what's the matter?"

"There's something completely wrong about the front end – the steering. It's not going to work for the SS's body design"

She looked at me and smiled. "I'm sure you'll find a way Howie. You always do. Just leave it for a while and carry on with something else. Something will come up," she told me, getting out of her chair and giving me a hug before heading to the kitchen. She was right of course. Like she always is.

That day, work continued on the chassis. I forced the steering fiasco from my mind and began to regain enthusiasm. I had made the decision to put my other work on the back-burner for a couple of days and get my teeth into the SS project – I needed to see some progress.

Now, as mentioned earlier in the piece, I'd already designed my version of the chassis, so apart from the rear end, which, as opposed to the original, has a raised section to accommodate coil springs rather than ellipticals, I simply followed the dimensions on the drawing Brett had given me. So, happily, by the end of the day, I stood in the middle of the floor sucking on a cold beer gazing down on two seriously nice looking chassis rails, all tacked together, angles etc. correct and ready for the next phase, which would involve laying them on the trestles, bolted to the floor and perfectly level. I would set them up by welding in some dummy cross-members to keep them the correct distance apart while I dealt with ancillary brackets and mountings etc. Feeling very pleased and big headed, I headed home to tell Gail about it – we may even go out to dinner tonight, to celebrate. How childish! But I was elated to see something material. Peter would be in tomorrow and would no doubt insert his two bob.

"Well!" I announced happily "I've built the two chassis rails today." I kissed the lady.

"That's nice Howie," she said. "Did you remember to get the cat food and potatoes on your way home?"

I love women, but boy are they good at whipping the wind out of your sails, I thought sourly. Isn't that nice. I come home with glad tidings and all she's interested in is cat food and potatoes.

"Bugger! I'm sorry. I forgot!"

"Never mind."

"Let's go to the Jenna Tavern for a steak – how about that my Baby?"

She's never been known to refuse a meal at the Jenna, so off we went that evening. The Jennacubine Tavern is 26km away from Northam, deep inside the bush. The last thing you would expect to find at the end of a long narrow dark road (mind the kangaroos) is a steakhouse. Drive, drive, drive. Suddenly, lights in the bush and you are there. People come from afar and stay over at this place, just to indulge in the best steaks in the State. That night was no exception.

I slept the sleep of the dead and woke up refreshed, bright and bushy tailed at 6 o'clock. Then I headed for the mechanical gardens for what would be.

CHATPER SEVEN

THE ENGINE The days, weeks and months following my inroads with the chassis, produced a spike in my workload at H&G Engineering, resulting in only sporadic bursts of activity on the SS – much to my frustration, but we have to earn a crust. However, much progress was made on researching components such as wheels (the story of which qualifies to encompass an entire chapter on its own), power unit, instrumentation, seats, lights and windscreen. During these busy times, one of the things I did achieve was to purchase an engine, complete with all ancillaries and full wiring harness.

What is it about motor wreckers that set them apart from other humans? Let me explain. First of all they, more often than not, own a dog the size of a Mack truck. So, when I visit one of these establishments, my priority (as readers will imagine) is to study the surroundings and make sure there is something to climb. Secondly, after ringing the inevitable bell on the service desk, the guy that appears is almost always a big sod, inside an oily pair of overalls, carrying a spanner in a threatening manner and looking as pissed off as their dog. The fella that greeted me at All Ford Spares in Bayswater seemed no different to the stereotype. Sure enough, he turned up at the front desk with an accusing look on his face – no spanner – only a starter motor tucked in the crook of his elbow. I expected him to say, "What the fuck do you want?" but his face broke into a broad friendly smile.

"Good morning," he offered.

"Hi."

"Whatcha chasing?" he enquired politely.

"I'm looking for a late model Ford engine – low kilometres if possible…what's your name mate?"

"I'm Lee – the owner!" Then he continued without allowing me to reciprocate. "These engines are all different. It all depends on what you're chucking it into. What are you going to do with it?"

"I'm building a replica of a pre-war sports car!"

"Oh yeah," Lee said leaning on the counter now, placing the starter motor down and showing an expression of interest. "What pre-war car?"

"It's a Jaguar SS100 – 1937!"

Lee sucked in most of the air around his head and whistled. "You're pretty bloody brave," he grinned. "But I've got something for you. Let's go out back." Lee led the way into the backyard. "Careful as you go," he warned as we negotiated the normal minefield of precarious looking piles of bodies, suspensions, diffs and myriad other bits. We ended our journey next to a Falcon ute sporting bad left front damage. "This is what you want mate – what did you say your name was?"

"I didn't – Howie is my name – short for Howard."

"Ok Howie, this ute's done 109,000km – very quickly it seems – as you can see she's like new."

"No damage to the engine?"

"Only a dent in the sump, nothing else," he answered then added, "I warranty these anyway."

I looked inside. Just as I thought, it was an automatic. That was alright, I had other plans anyway.

As if reading my mind, Lee ventured. "You'd probably want a manual for your job though."

"I do. What I'm building wouldn't do as an automatic I'm afraid, but I have a plan. I'm using a four-speed Volvo gearbox. That way it'll be more authentic."

He pulled a wry face. "You also may run into trouble doing that! I believe the automatic's computer isn't compatible with a manual gearbox. You'll have to change the computer. I know guys who are having trouble chopping and changing in racing circles. The engines run rich as buggery and they can't seem to sort it – so be careful," he concluded.

"Fair enough, can you provide the other computer? Are they hard to find?"

"They are, but they are available – and expensive."

"Well, if that's what is going to solve the problem, then that's what we will do." We made our way back to the front chatting about the project I was doing and Lee asked lots of intelligent questions and even offered me some handy tips, which I stored away somewhere in the old grey matter.

"Do you want the motor?" he enquired.

"Sure. Sure. As long as it still runs good."

"Oh, it will. We'll test it before you go so you can listen." He told me reassuringly.

So that's what we did. Lee connected a battery pack to the ute and started it up. It ran smoothly and silently – nothing sinister here.

"I'm happy with that." I told him. "How much?"

"Let's go back up front." He led the way.

Back at the counter, he looked at me and said, "I'm going to give you a special price. I'm going to let you have the engine – you don't need the gearbox – and the complete wiring harness for $1100. How does that sound?"

"That sounds fine to me," I told him. Then money changed hands and Lee told me the motor would be ready for pickup in a couple of days.

"I'll keep in touch," I said on my way out, heading back to Northam.

Getting back to the chassis, as mentioned earlier, I'd constructed it to the dimensions and geometry of the original. Apart from the kick-up at the rear, looking at a front elevation of a longitudinal member, starting at the rear, it runs level for a while then angles upward until it reaches a point where the front cross-member is connected. This levels off again to accommodate same and after that, heads off downhill till the end, in the area where the louvered apron lives. One day, I was standing next to the dusty cobwebbed front end, with the steering box still clamped in position. But I was not looking at that. I was looking at the chassis, and a thought occurred to me.

Heights!

I had done no accurate calculations as to the exact ride heights – although it had looked pretty close. So, out came the measuring sticks, string, straight edge and calculator. First, I drew a simulation of the rear end connected to hypothetical mountings and calculated that with 18" wheels and cross-ply tyres, a distance of 240mm from the underside of the chassis to the road could be achieved. This scenario would produce a chassis that rode approximately 40mm higher than the original. While acutely aware that this car's general presence could be impaired by sitting too high off the ground, I did feel that 40mm may not be too much. So that was okay. I was happy with that.

Not for long.

I went to the front. There was a string-line set up to indicate the difference in height between the underside of the chassis rail at the rear and the point where the front cross-member fitted. I pressed some buttons and came up with a figure – looking good, about what I had in mind. Then, over to the cross-member on the floor. Measure the distance from the mounting point at the top, down to the hub centre. The springs were in position, so this measurement would be correct with no load. Fair enough. Press more buttons. I came up with an answer. To my horror, I see that the car would be 100mm higher at the front than the rear. I hurriedly went through the exercise again, this time taking the lower 'A' Arm to be standing level with the road. This would be the maximum the suspension could drop, without running out of springing altogether. Still, the calculator told me the car would be 50mm higher at the front.

Shit!

An empty 20-litre paint tin sat on the concrete floor near where I was standing. I walked across and sat down on it, gazing dejectedly at the chassis, but not seeing it. No, I was looking straight through it. There was no excuse for this – no excuse at all. I was no mechanic or car body builder – I knew that. Just a toolmaker – but still something of an engineer. But had I been a florist, there would still have been no excuse for making a fundamental blunder like this. And I'd only just started! My mind wandered for a while back into the mists of the past – to around 1967 and to something that a wise old tradesman by the name of Andy Skurving had told me.

"My boy. There's only one thing worse than an idiot. That's an enthusiastic one." I've never forgotten that. Or had I? Earlier in the piece, I referred to myself as an enthusiastic amateur. Perhaps I was being too kind.

I sat there for a long time, taking stock of things as they stood. I was pissed off with myself…and fearful too. Those butterflies began gnawing at me again. Maybe I wasn't up to this after all. But the idea of chucking in the towel and giving it away was too much for my ego to bear. I had committed. Finally, I made a promise to myself. I would find a way to fix this and then call a halt to all further construction until everything had been thoroughly researched.

Peter turned up the next day for a coffee. I broke the news to him and cried on his shoulder.

"Holy fuck," he uttered with a grimace after I'd explained.

"A right mess, isn't it?"

"You're not wrong!" Then he began pacing up and down in front of and around the chassis, as if that would help. At length, he came over and looked quizzically at me and asked "Could you break the chassis and increase the climb towards the front? That would lower it!" I'd already thought about that.

"Good thinking Peter – but I'm afraid it won't work. John Byfield is building the wings on the Boughtons' jigs. They won't fit if I do that. I thought about it last night," I concluded.

"Bugger. You're right," he agreed. "We'll think of something."

After gum-flapping for a while, Peter shot through. After he left, I was about to start the surface grinder up, when suddenly an idea came to me. If I cut 50mm out of the underside of the RHS at the point where the cross-member bolts on, then I would just about get away with it. Some fancy reinforcing would be required – but how would this be viewed by an engineer? I did some paperwork and my calculations assured me that if I performed a bit of overkill, there would be no reason for an engineer to fail it on strength.

So, out came the angle grinder and I got stuck in.

CHAPTER EIGHT

GIFTS AND BAD TIDINGS It was wintertime again in Northam and as cold as ever in the valley. The SS project was a year old now and I hadn't yet employed an engineer to give me the shits. This needed to be done, so one afternoon I unearthed the paperwork supplied to me by Technical in Welshpool where I'd first registered the project. Browsing through a list of engineers recommended by the department, my finger came to rest on a certain gentleman's name (whom I will hereafter refer to as 'Mr Katz'). He sounded as good as any, so I rang him. Once I'd outlined what I was up to, he asked a number of questions relating to the build and also about me. It felt like I was the subject of an interrogation. Subtlety wasn't this prick's most shining attribute I remember thinking at the time.

"It depends on the attitude of the builder," he had pointed out, "and there are time wasters out there. I've had problems in the past – especially with ICVs, so these days I'm a bit fussy about what I take on. Sorry to be negative but that's just the way it is," he concluded.

Geez! This party sounded like your classic 'glass half-empty type'. "Fair enough," I said curtly, expecting the conversation to be terminated now. "If you're not interested, can you point me in the direction of someone who possibly would be?"

"Oh no – don't get me wrong. I'm interested. I like the concept," he allowed, quickly changing his tone.

"Okay, so do you want the job?"

"Yes."

"So, what comes next?"

"I will come to you and see what your plans are," he told me, then added, "have you done anything yet?"

"Yes I have. Most of the chassis is complete…"

He interrupted me, now sounding annoyed. "You shouldn't have done that – how do you know it'll pass a stress test?"

Cheeky sod. So I bit back. "I don't. That's your job. The cruciform and cross-members haven't been done yet. I've purposely left them out for that reason and the chassis rails are overkill at 100x50x3 RHS."

I thought I heard what sounded like a faint giggle at the other end of the line and Katz said: "Okay – we'll see! He then made arrangements to call on me and I went back to work. I was taking a slice off the cylinder head from an old CB750 Honda. I'd only just turned the machine back on when a familiar voice boomed across the workshop. I switched it off.

To my surprise, Harry Levenstein had materialised in the doorway. "Hey Boofhead."

I looked at my watch. "Harry, what the hell are you doing in Northam?" It was mid-afternoon. "Aren't you supposed to be attending to your victims?"

"Shut up you," he retorted and walked over. We shook hands.

"How are you cobber. Long time no see. What's been happening?"

"I went to South Africa."

"Oh yeah – good?"

"Yes. Very nice break thank you." He was carrying a small cardboard box – what did he want me to do now? I wondered vaguely.

"I took a drive out to Isando while I was with relatives on the West Rand and dropped in on Willy." Harry was wearing an impish grin now. "Open the box," he said passing it to me.

Opening the box, I removed the contents and unwrapped a set of four shiny period bonnet catches just perfect for the SS, and to top it all, they were brand new. Wow!

"An early Christmas present." Harry's beady little black eyes peered over his glasses at me. "Don't expect anything else."

"Aha, you went to the SS guy in Jo'burg." "Well done mate. Thank you! Thank you! Something I won't have to chase down now."

He looked pleased. "Willy's operation is quite impressive. His daughter's the engine assembler in his factory. She's the only certified Jaguar engine builder in South Africa – according to him. I watched her in action for a while. Interesting. Now, I asked him about headlights for your SS – and taillights for that matter. Willy told me their dies for the taillights are still in the tool room. Oh yes, and I brought a price list from him too. You are in for a surprise my boy! How does three thousand dollars sound for a radiator cowl? That's chromed with the mesh but no dog-bone cap."

"Good Heavens! I could never afford that – I can see myself having to make a lot of these parts myself you know Harry."

"Why don't you ask that chap in England, the one that builds the Suffolk SS. He may be able to help," Harry offered.

"Yeah. I'll talk to him," I mumbled and turned the milling machine back on.

We stood there gasbagging for a while then Harry finally noticed the chassis up on the stands and trudged across. "You've been busy son."

"Not busy enough!" I yelled above the clatter of an interrupted cut on the mill.

He came back over and asked: "What are those Suffolk SS cars like Howie, do you know?"

"I really don't know anything about them, apart from the fact that he uses XJ6 running gear, brakes, suspension etc. As far as I know they have automatic transmissions. They are fiberglass though, but I think the bonnet and some other parts are aluminium."

"I wonder what the build quality is like," Harry said casually. "I don't mind the automatic personally – depends on individual preferences."

"The cars look beautiful though. Get on the internet and check out his website. It's a hard act to follow."

"What do they cost?"

"No idea – oi – what are you thinking?"

"No, no, no!" he waved me away, "just interested!"

"Yeah, yeah." Then he gave me a friendly slap on the back and turned to go. "I have to keep moving Howie. Keep up the good work. I have an appointment in Chidlow!" Then Harry jumped into his puddle jumper and drove off.

I tried again. Once the cylinder head was finished, it was time to have a cuppa and I sat down thinking about the next job. As I rose to get started, the guy who owned the Honda cylinder head came in. Phew! Talk about timing. He paid for the job and before departing he spied my bits scattered around and asked the inevitable question.

I explained and then he said: "My neighbour is a tinsmith by trade. His name is Alec. You may want to have a look at what he is doing in his shed. I haven't had a close look, but it seems to be a similar thing to yours. It looks around the same era."

"Really. That's interesting – I wonder what it is? Where do you guys live?"

"Spencers Brook…if you like, I'll give you Alec's number. The old boy is very approachable and ten to one he'll want to chat, seeing the two of you have a common interest."

"I would appreciate that – and I will certainly contact him. Thank you."

He wrote the number on a 'post-it-note'.

"Who knows, I may be able to learn something?"

So off he went with his cylinder head and I stuck the 'post-it-note' with Alec's number on my wall – happy as Larry to have another potential contact. I would speak to this Alec real soon. I wondered how far down the track he was? I wonder what it was? As the afternoon wore on, being who I was, the curiosity of what was going on just below the horizon in Spencers Brook overtook my waning interest in the job I was doing. So I did the most sensible thing at the time.

"Alec speaking!" a polite sounding voice announced.

CHAPTER NINE

OUT OF THE BLUE & A STRANGE ENCOUNTER "Howie Pietersie Alec. A fella I did a job for today gave me your number. He said you're up to some kind of mischief in your shed!" I said laughingly and he laughed too.

"Oh – the Mercedes you mean?"

"I didn't know that. A Mercedes eh!"

"Yes. I'm trying to build a replica 1928 model Roadster."

"Wow! That sounds fantastic!" I uttered excitedly trying hard to sound like I knew what a 1928 Mercedes looked like. "Any chance of me coming to have a look? Sorry Alec, I'm being pushy – hey reason be known, I'm also building something. A 1937 SS Jaguar!"

"Certainly you can come and look. Where are you Howie? You in Northam?"

"Yep. I have a factory unit on Yilgarn Avenue, opposite Midalia Steel."

"My place is in Spencers Brook. I'm about half an hour away from coming into town. Maybe I'll drop in and see you first. I'd love to see your project too."

"Magic Alec!" I told him. "It's Unit 3, 12 Yilgarn Ave. I'll be here until about six mate. Look forward to meeting you." Well, how about that! It was good to know that just down the road somebody else was also in need of a brain operation – nothing like safety in numbers. Possibly ten minutes after I'd opened the fridge that afternoon, a tall, well built, proud looking grey haired figure with glasses materialised in the doorway of my unit.

I approached. "Alec?"

"Howie! – good to meet you."

We stood chatting and exchanging informative titbits about our respective projects, and then Alec had a look at my chassis and the running gear dotted around the floor.

"What are you doing about the body panels Howie? Will you build them yourself?" he asked.

"At this stage Alec, apart from the wings mate – yes. Although, for me, it won't be easy. You see, I still have to learn how to do these things. This is my first attempt at building a car. I have no idea how things will go with forming up body panels and all I can do is try, I guess. Take the doors for instance!" I pointed at the little silver model. "I'm terrified of them, never mind the rest of it!"

"If you like, when I go home, I'll do a mock up – a little one, to show you roughly how to construct a door."

"Will you really? That is most kind of you. Any help I can get will be welcome to say the least."

And then he went away and so help me, the very next morning, he showed up again with the sample piece. A piece of 18-guage galvanized sheet about 250mm square it was, with the bottom corner opposite the hinged end, neatly radiused as per the SS. All the various little nips and folds demonstrating the correct method of constructing a door had been meticulously crafted. It looked great and cleared up some of my concerns about building the doors. I took the item out of his hands and turned it over a few times, impressed by the professional way it had been made.

I looked at him and said, "I'm very grateful for this Alec. Thank you."

Our world is still teeming with wonderful, kind humans you know! How about this man? How many people would go out of their way to do something like this for a complete stranger? A clear and powerful comradeship exists between those who dedicate themselves to projects such as these. Alec, the Boughtons, Frank, John Byfield. There would be more times like this. I knew it. Surrounded by all these wonderful people, how could I fail? Every time I thought about building this weird shaped skeleton, encompassing the tub–scuttle, I wondered how on earth I would be able to make the doors fit it. They had compound curves and radii that all needed to blend into each other and then still fit the skeleton. It was too much for the brain. But suddenly – wait a minute! Why do I have to do it that way around? Why not build the doors first – get them as close as possible to Brett's doors and then build the skeleton around them!

A cop out? Yes – a cop out – but if it works, so what! I decided then to have a go at the doors in-between times.

The following day, I was distracted by a very important telephone call. "H&G Engineering, Howie speaking!"

"Hi Howie – this is John Byfield – how would you like to pick up your mudguards?"

"So you've finished them John. Hooray man! Well done. Unfortunately, I can't get there for about a week. I will ring before I come," I told him excitedly. I can't remember what I told him at the time as to why it would be a week before I travelled down to pick them up, but the truth was I still owed him a few thousand dollars and I was waiting on some money to come in.

Brett Boughton had rung that day to let me know that there was a car show at a venue in South Perth on the weekend and he was taking 'Miss SS100' for an outing.

"You may feel like a drive down Howie."

"May! I'll be there with bells my friend," I told him enthusiastically. Anything for another chance to have a sticky beak around the white SS.

"Bring your measuring tape!" he laughed.

I laughed. "I will mate." And I did.

At the show, Brett's car was perched at the top of a grass mound, in front of a marquee, the proud owner standing beside her in appropriate attire, complete with period cap. People were milling around the lady and Brett was kept busy answering questions and carrying on polite conversation with interested people. I gave him a wide berth, just waved hello and took more photos of the car. Later, when the people had moved on, I chatted with him and then, feeling a little conspicuous, took nominal sizes of the right-hand door. That would be enough info to get me started on a mock-up. I went for a walk around the show and saw that there was another SS100 in the rows of Jaguars. It was a cream colour and the owner was standing alongside it. I struck up a conversation with him.

"Howie Pietersie's my name!" I offered a hand.

He reciprocated. "Gill Peters."

"Hi Gill. Is this a real SS or a replica?"

He glanced at me sharply as if I should have known – well, I didn't.

"It's a replica."

"Oh, very nice." I offered. "I'm building a lookalike."

"A lookalike? How do you mean?"

"Well, different running gear – that's all. Hopefully the rest will be the same. So Gill, did you build the replica?" I asked him, trying to steer the conversation away from my car's running gear.

But he wasn't having any of that. "So, what's the chassis and what engine are you using?"

"Oh! The chassis is as per the original etc., and Volvo suspension and brakes," I added.

"Volvo! But don't you think that will be detrimental to the value of the car? What about the engine?"

"I'm still working on that Gill. Not sure yet."

"If I were you, I would stick to Jaguar stuff man. Using anything else, if you try to sell it one day, you'd get bugger all for it," he concluded.

"That bad hey! Still – I suppose we can't all have the good stuff. I may just have to settle for a sub-standard vehicle and be happy with it. Anyway, I had never thought about the resale. Money doesn't mean much to me mate!"

He just stood looking blankly at me and with that, I wished him well and continued my tour of the show in ever decreasing circles, finishing up with Brett again. Soon I said goodbye and went on my way.

CHAPTER TEN

A SPANNER IN THE WORKS Now, some months earlier, John Byfield had mentioned the name of a gentleman who was known around the traps to peddle hard to get bits for old Jaguars. This was one Terry McGrath – apparently an active member of the local Jaguar Club. John had given me his number.

"Terry will most probably be able to help you with things like instruments," he had said.

So one day I contacted Mr McGrath and told him what I was up to – but purposely avoided discussing the concept of my creation. One never can tell what reaction I may get once I divulged that my car would be so far removed from the real thing!

"Hi Terry – I'm Howie Pietersie. There's a rumour going around that you may be able to help me with old Jaguar parts. I'm in the process of building an SS100 lookalike."

"Oh! Hello. Yes I could possibly help you." He didn't waste much time in peeling me back. "What chassis are you using?" he asked curiously.

"I'm not, Terry – I'm building the chassis!"

"You won't be able to get it licensed. You need to start with an old chassis and rebuild the car. That way it will legally be a restoration and the Department will allow it on the road."

"But I've been through all that with the Technical Section in Welshpool, and I'm okay to build the car as an individually constructed vehicle. Anyhow, I'll see how things go!" I quickly changed the subject and added. "Could you help me find some instruments?"

"Yes, I can supply you a complete set of gauges and at a reasonable cost," he informed me, then reverted back to the chassis thing. "I have got a chassis for you too. Listen – what engine are you going to use?"

"Oh! I haven't thought about that yet," I lied.

"Well, talk to me when the time comes – but please, don't go down the track you're on. You will have problems. Believe me!"

"Well, okay. I'll think about what you've said Terry. And thanks for the advice. I will be in touch about the instrumentation."

With that, the conversation ended and I was left standing with the phone in my hand and mixed feelings. Maybe he was right. Maybe I should have thought more carefully about this whole thing. No question about it, there was merit in what McGrath had told me. Something deep inside was telling me to listen to him. Take the easy way out. I would avoid all those nasties, such as emissions control, warning lights for everything, seatbelts, etc. And above all, endless lists of components that would require engineering tests and reports. But if I did what he was suggesting, in my tiny mind that would translate into a cop-out! The intention always was to build a car. Build a car – not start with an existing chassis. That concept took too much away from my vision. Besides, I was harbouring a dark secret. Preposterous as it may seem, or may have seemed at the time, if this project did work – and work well – an entire drivable, body-less vehicle could easily be replicated, for others. Perhaps I could build a few more myself. Who knows! Delusions of grandeur? Crazy eh? Maybe not! Any thoughts of Howie Pietersie and his weird ideas would surely have perished in Terry McGrath's mind seconds after ringing off – I'm sure. But late, late that night, when McGrath was sleeping peacefully, I was still dwelling on our discussion. My heart would lead the way – and it did – straight back on the road I was on.

A few days after the talk with Terry, I hooked up a trailer and made my way to Kent Street, where John Byfield's hangout was. They were in the lunch room – John and Stan – reading newspapers and having morning tea. After smoko, John showed me his handiwork. The two front wings were clamped together so that I could compare their profiles to one another. They looked good to me. Because they had been crafted remote to the car, he had sensibly left the part of the front wings that attach to the car, unfinished. The intention being that I take them back home, get it all set up roughly in the correct position, and report back to him. Then we would arrange for John to pay a visit to Northam.

I also had pre-arranged for Brett and Ian to come along too. They were both eager to have a look. But at that time, the great man had skipped the country – with Miss SS110 and was gallivanting around Asian racetracks showing the locals how it's done. So I had to wait for him to come home before setting a date for their visit. For obvious reasons, I was apprehensive about that. What would they think? Was I doing okay? Peter had turned up one morning and asked me to do a small job on the lathe. While we were standing around sipping cups of coffee and gasbagging about the usual stuff, I was gazing at the cross-member with the steering box still clamped to it. The entire thing was covered in dust and cobwebs, as it had been for months.

Peter looked at it too and pointed. He smiled at me and said: "What's going to happen about that?"

I answered immediately – mainly because it just came to me in the instant. "Somehow I'm going to fit a rack and pinion system Peter. It's the only answer."

"Holy…" he uttered. "Where would you put the rack – this thing steers from the front Howie." He walked over and bent down next to the cross-member. He stared at it for a while then turned to face me. "If you did manage to fit a rack to the front somehow, you'll have to find a way to feed the movement over the top of the cross-member!"

"I dunno Peter – I dunno!" I laughed. "But I'm sure I'll find a way. I have to do it. It's the only way. I'm certainly not changing the front end – that really would open a can of worms!" I told him emphatically.

"Good luck mate!" Peter said with a parting grin as he shot through. "You'll find a way. See you next week."

Now all you Einsteins out there would surely be laughing up your sleeves by now.

The penny finally dropped.

"Why did it take him so long to figure that out?

Well guys, that's just the point. At the time I simply did not know enough about that stuff. Come to think of it – Peter hadn't thought of that either. Or perhaps he had but never mentioned it because of the geometrical challenges that were involved. In any event, I rolled up my sleeves so to speak, and got heavily involved with the steering system again. It felt good – I would conquer. First it was cleaned up and lifted onto a table, then I began taking measurements, to see if it was feasible to build a housing onto the front of the cross-member to carry a rack and then transfer the movement over the top and find its way to the steering column by way of universal joints. It looked like I might just get away with it, so the next thing I did was to clamp the entire arrangement to the chassis and see where things would finish up. I soldiered on. Next, I procured some literature from the local library on the fundamentals of rack and pinion systems. Specifically, how to design them. I studied the contents of this information until I was crystal clear on how to go about this conversion. Over the next two weeks, I spent some time in wrecking yards, talking to big people with big dogs, armed with my measuring tape, until I found something that looked like it would do the job if I shortened it. This was a non-power steering rack and pinion from a Holden VL Commodore. I purchased this and headed home.

Back at the shop, I fabricated a cardboard mock-up of a housing at the front – top of the cross-member that would house the rack and pinion and also double as a radiator mount. That worked, so I built a metal one. Then, after painstakingly calculating and re-calculating the relative positions of the ball joints on the rack and 'A' arms, because if this was not correct, bump steer would occur and we couldn't have that – could we? Apparently, if this occurs, every time you hit a bump, the steering jolts! Not a pleasant thought. By the time this job was finished it actually looked very professional and I felt quite proud of myself. I wondered what the engineer would think?

So! Problem solved! I would carry on with something else now. Yes! We were making steady progress.

CHAPTER ELEVEN

A CHANGE OF DIRECTION By the time the day came for the 'Three Wise Men' from Perth to come up, the status of the project was as follows:

The chassis was almost complete with the exception of the cruciform and one or two other minor details. The front and rear ends were in temporarily. The guards were clamped in position, ready for John Byfield to do his magic. The engine was in place, perched on a drum and I had begun fabricating the skeleton around the tub.

Katz had approved all the reinforcing plates and engine mounting brackets I had made up, but told me I wasn't able to final weld them as the law called for someone who was suitably qualified to do the job (which was probably just as well!). Years before, while operating a business in Wangara and after advertising for a welder/boilermaker, I finished up interviewing and subsequently engaging a young Englishman from Middlesborough, one Adam Rout. Prior to migrating to Australia, Adam had worked at the Triumph factory in England, welding up motorcycle frames, among other things.

Over the years, Gail and I had cultivated a strong friendship with Adam and his lovely German lady Isabella, which persists to the present day. Rumour had it that Adam could arc weld american cedar to pewter with an aluminium rod, so I invited him to weld up all the chassis bits. Katz was suitably impressed with the result and declared the chassis and ancillaries well within his expectations. Another job done.

Yippee! So back to the Three Wise Men.

The snout of our LS400 was blocking the mouth of the workshop, so the V8 Soarer snuck up the side of the Lexus. The first I knew was when the three of them appeared in the shop.

Ian Boughton was the first to speak. He shook my hand vigorously and strode straight over to the car – or better still, what was showing definite signs of turning into one. "You've fucking cracked it!" he uttered in his best workshop language. While he continued investigating, Brett, John and I exchanged greetings, then went over to join Ian. It was on after that. They were like a bunch of termites – twisting, bending and peering under things. Asking questions, offering advice, and to my great relief and surprise, showed genuine admiration for my workmanship so far. Suddenly, after feelings of apprehension bordering on fear, I felt ten feet tall – No! – eleven feet tall. All the while, John Byfield was preparing to take sizes etc. on the guards so that I could bring them back to him for finishing work.

Brett tugged at my sleeve and indicated to John: "Watch him – they don't need measuring tapes – they strike chalk marks, these old guys!" We checked him out. He was peering at the guards from many angles and would then stick a chalk mark. At one point, he stood in front of the car peering down the chassis line for a good three minutes, cocking his head to one side, then the other. He looked like he was checking the rifling in the barrel of an old World War II .303. Once he'd eyeballed a point, he'd quickly go over and strike another chalk mark. A true craftsman at work. Wow! Having these boys here was a real high point for me. It was confidence inspiring. I felt so happy.

Now, John and Brett were yapping about something, and while this was going on, Ian came around from the driver's side of the car. He wore an expression I hadn't seen before. A kind of worried, guilty, yet amused look – if you can imagine that. I won't forget it. Then he stood alongside me and spoke in subdued tones, out of the corner of his mouth, like he didn't want the other two to hear. I was puzzled.

"I just turned the shaft on your steering rack cobber – it's going the wrong way!"

Well, needless to say – my blood just about froze in my veins. I descended into panic – cold, unforgiving panic! Here was a classic case of 'can't see the wood for the trees'. Unbelievable, only a year before, I'd been chatting to a guy from Leeds, who had done exactly the same thing on a Mini! And he was a mechanic.

Holy crap!!!

Amid all the geometrical calculations in the process of getting this to work, this glaring fact had escaped me. What the @#$%*ing hell was I going to do now? I started to laugh – out loud. Then Ian joined in and the others quickly demanded we share the joke. Then we were all laughing. I was so embarrassed. And it was agreed by all that I was a strong contender for some exotic award, such as 'Prick of the Year'.

Oh dear!

I knew then that I would be designing and building a reversing gearbox to change the direction. Even as we stood there, my mind was conjuring up images as to how I would build a reversing gearbox. I would find a way. The boys headed back to Perth and I went home and confessed to my lady.

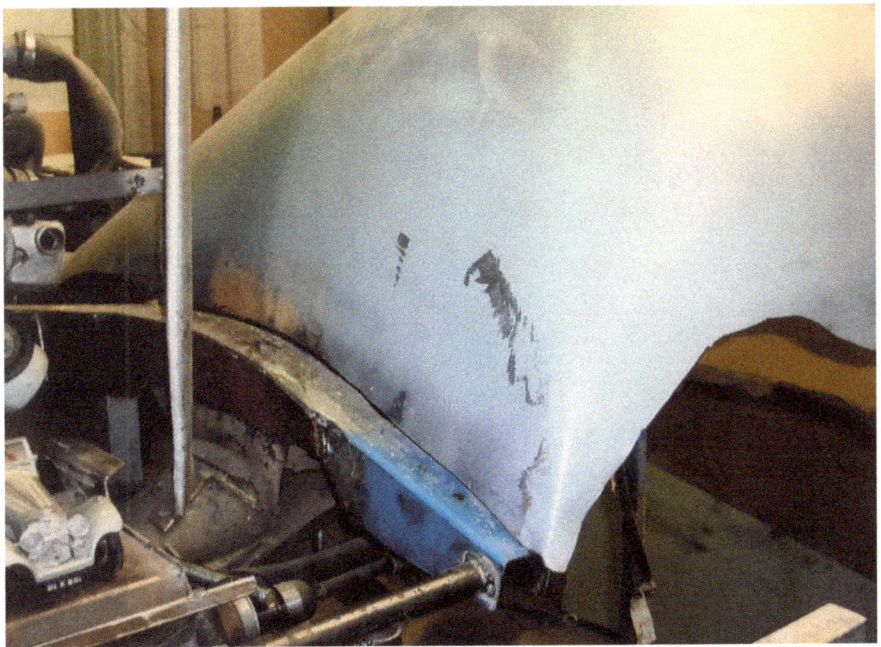

PART TWO

CHAPTER TWELVE

ENGAGING GEARS Before beginning the task of fixing my monumental cock-up on the steering, it occurred to me that I should talk with the engineer about the reversing unit first, in case the concept turned out to be illegal. But what would he think? I felt embarrassed about my oversight. I decided rather than approaching Katz about it, a chat with Bob at Technical might clear up the legal aspect of things. So I rang him.

Once he had finished laughing at me, he offered the following observation: "Howie, providing the unit you fit is of sound design and is mounted correctly and your engineer accepts its integrity, you will have no problem with us." Then he added: "Anyway, I've seen your set-up and truth be known, it would have been near impossible to find a rack that fitted your design without having to make some kind of major changes. So, doing it your way and reversing the direction makes perfect engineering sense as far as I can see – so just go into your workshop and design something up. As long as your engineer passes it, there will be no problem."

Bob and I chatted for a while and he suggested a couple of calls to some of the hot rod clubs in case somebody in their circles had experienced a similar situation. "That way you may get something off the shelf," he ventured.

"Good idea Bob," I said. "I will try that." Soon after, I rang off, feeling better about things. Later that day, after attending to a farmer who needed a couple of bronze bushes made, I sat down with a cup of tea and reflected on my conversation with Bob. The comments he had made about the difficulties finding a rack and pinion made sense, and I realised to my horror that my whole embarrassing situation had not needed to take place at all. Had my tiny brain been capable of some quick thinking the day my three wise men had visited, I could have turned things around and instead of feeling like a complete fucking idiot, it may have gone something like this:

I could have laughed when Ian had mentioned the direction and said:

"Oh that. I was wondering when you were going to pick that up. Unfortunately finding a rack that would sit in the correct position and accommodate the front facing steering arms, was near impossible so I've had to incorporate a reversing gearbox to change the direction. I'll fit it at the base of the steering column."

But I'm just not switched on enough people! Just not switched on enough – or too honest? So there you go. Enthusiastic amateur – or enthusiastic idiot – you choose! Enough already, move on!

"No! Sorry cob. You'll be struggling there. All our units are 90° boxes. And anyway, they are all redirection boxes and you would need one to one." The guy I was speaking with was the fourth of his kind in as many hours. Pneumatic companies, power transmission people and even kit car and hot rod clubs had all turned up negative, and lastly this guy, who supplied gearboxes for chemical dosing systems.

"Okay Sir," I acknowledged dismally, "I'll keep trying." But by then I'd had enough.

It was 'beer o'clock' – I cracked one and began padding aimlessly around the workshop and rummaging around amongst a growing hoard of motorcycle odds and sods, looking for I don't know what, when I spied an old Yamaha XT250 bottom end. The clutch cover had been removed years before, and getting up close and personal, I noticed the crankshaft gear. This could be a starting point. Dragging it out, I dropped it onto the workbench and inspected the teeth. The gear was in good condition. If I could unearth another one the same… Once I'd removed the gear and cleaned it up, I made a note of the dimensions and number of teeth, with the intention of having a ring around the wreckers, but glancing at the wall clock, I saw that it was after five and my calls would have to wait until the morning.

I decided that before coming to work the next day, a visit to our local motorbike shop was in order. Maybe Kim Read had something.

"G'day Kim," I greeted once I found him around the back, pressure washing a motocross bike.

He switched the machine off.

"How's Howie?"

"Good Kim – how about you?"

"No point grumbling – what's up?"

I liked Kim. He was a good operator. Good at his job and always helpful. He was also, at the time, the president of the local motocross club and an excellent rider too. I pressed the gear into his hand and smiled at him.

"What's this for?" he queried.

"It's from an XT250. I'm chasing another one the same. "Will I get lucky? It's the crankshaft gear."

"You never know." He led the way through a side door and we entered a shed. I didn't realise he had this area. The place was packed to the rafters with naked bike frames. Some with engines, some without. Myriad boxes and bucket loads of brake discs, sprockets and cables hung off the walls.

Kim's eyes swept around the place until they came to rest on one particular box buried under three or four others. "There may be one in there," he said. I gave a hand and presently we were sorting through dozens of gears. Then Kim suggested I keep on searching while he carried on with his work. Not five minutes later, I emerged wearing a triumphant grin and after paying the princely sum of $10 for an identical gear, I headed off to work.

The steering column from the Volvo was, by now, in position and held fast with temporary mountings. A universal joint at the end of the shaft finished up in a convenient position nicely between the engine block and chassis rail. A mounting bracket at the inside of the chassis rail for the reversing unit to live on would do the trick. Next came some sketches. Exciting stuff! Forget everything else…I sat at my desk with the two gears in front of me and nutted out a design. The gears were just perfect for the job (albeit overkill) – 25 diameter shafts, bearings and circlips. Each block had 50mm of shaft protruding from one side to take the universals and the two blocks were married up so that the gears meshed just enough to achieve the correct amount of backlash. Fuck I'm good! Yea! Yea!

It took four days before the aluminium blocks turned up, but when they did I dropped what I was doing at the time like a sack of potatoes and got into it. The initial sketches I'd made had turned into accurate drawings and so there was no second guessing myself. The job was started at 10 o'clock and I worked furiously until finally when beer o'clock arrived, the little reversing box was complete and perched on my desk. It looked professional and worked perfectly. I felt good about doing something right for a change. I needed it for ego repair. I went home and broke the good news to Gail.

Time was wearing on, and more than two years had passed the door by the summer of 2007 and much progress was evident looking at the SS. Multiple trips to Canning Vale checking and re-checking dimensions on the Boughton masterpiece were behind me, and over the time I gained useful information investigating supply lines for components such as headlights, wheels, tyres, windscreen and odds and ends like bonnet catches, mirrors, door hinges etc.

One Sunday morning Gail was helping me collate some kind of chronological order for the hopelessly confusing mound of photos and notes I had amassed since beginning the project, when we heard the sound of motorbikes pulling up outside the house. By this time we had moved house. That was a story in itself, but I'll keep it short.

One lovely Saturday around midday I pulled the Rover out for a run and with no particular destination in mind, went mooching around the backstreets of Northam, sort of crisscrossing my way towards the west end of town. Along the way, as usual, I stopped to peer through gaps in fences and gates in case something interesting lurked on the other side. Once suburbia began to peter out, I found myself heading back towards town down Fitzgerald Street. Opposite the old railway station stands a gorgeous old double storey federation building, The Grand Hotel. I had driven past it numerous times noting that it was deserted and boarded up. But not today. The doors were open and a sign stood on the corner near the bar door – 'Grand Hotel Open'. Out of curiosity I pulled up. And before I had a chance to go inside, a man came out of the bar and approached me.

He introduced himself as Daniel and offered his hand. "Can I have a look at your Rover? It's beautiful!" The Rover never failed to attract attention.

"Sure, help yourself. I'm Howie. Are you the new owner of this place Daniel?" I asked while he had a look around the car.

"Yes I am. Come inside," he said, turning and beckoning me to follow. "I've got a fire going."

I followed him through the bar doors and was quite taken aback with the rich warm ambience inside the old building. To my right was a large restaurant-cum-function room and to the left, one of the best Jarrah bar counters I'd ever seen. Typical of the period, archways and stained glass panels abounded in the hallway adjoining the bar.

"Well, I had no idea this building was so nice inside," I commented to Daniel, who by now had gone behind the bar. I perched myself on a barstool opposite the fire.

"Yes it is nice, isn't it? I've spent the last nine months since I bought it, renovating." Daniel talked about having purchased the building as a project and told me of all his highs and lows along the way, while I sipped a light beer.

When I got home, I told Gail about my adventure. "He said they are doing a Sunday roast."

"So – that place is open again. You know Howie, that building is one of the prettiest in Northam. I've always loved the look of it." She mused.

"We can pop over for lunch tomorrow if you feel that way inclined, and you can see inside then," I suggested.

And so, for the next six months or so, Gail and I frequented the Grand for the odd beer or coffee and Sunday lunches. We became quite good friends with Daniel as well. One afternoon I slipped into the Grand on my way back from checking a job out in Cunderdin. Apart from Daniel behind the bar, the place was empty. He didn't look happy at all.

"What's the matter mate?" I enquired. "You look as though the bottom's fallen out of your world."

"Do you know anybody who wants to buy a pub?"

"What the…" this was very sudden. It took me by surprise.

"Things aren't working out Howie!" The story came out then that the two ladies who had been running the kitchen had left without notice and that the hotel was running at a loss which could not be sustained. "So, I have to shut the doors," he told me dejectedly.

"Hell Daniel, I'm so sorry to hear that." And I really was. Another broken dream I observed. So many in Northam.

I went home and told Gail about it. "After all the work and money he's sunk into the place."

She shook her head. "I feel for the man – I wish we could buy it Howie."

"There would be no point my Baby, it's a loss situation. We'd only get ourselves into trouble," I warned.

"But how about if we could get it at the right price and just close it down and use it as our home. You could have your workshop there too. Then you won't have to pay rent anymore either," she stated enthusiastically, her eyes lighting up.

"You like that old place, don't you lady?" I laughed.

"I love it. I feel so relaxed in that building. It's friendly."

My wife is the most unselfish human. Always considers my needs before hers. Constantly in our lives she has indulged me whatever I've wanted. Even the time, at age 50, I had the crazy idea to learn to ride a motocross bike and begin racing, she went along for the ride – which lasted twelve years. She seldom asks for anything. But when she does, if it's within my power to oblige, I will. But this was logical thinking too.

That same afternoon, I paid Daniel a visit.

CHAPTER THIRTEEN

BRASS AND GLASS So, I opened the door to see who had turned up on the motorbikes. It was Fred and Bob from Licensing.

"Hi guys!" It was always good to catch up with these two. "Brekky in York again?" I asked even though I knew full well they had been to the Triumph Restaurant.

"Yep, thought we'd come through this way and investigate. How's it coming along?" asked Bob with a smile.

"Oh, the SS. Yes, things are happening. Come through." We went inside and the boys said their hellos to Gail on the way through to the mechanical gardens, and after making a cuppa for them, we stood around chatting. Fred walked around the SS and as usual, tugged at things to see if he could detach them, while Bob had a look around to see if I had been working on the right side of the legal fence, so to speak.

"Fred! Stop fucking around with things mate – leave the car alone," Bob growled and I just laughed. Fred was good at this. I remember walking around with him at a car show some years before and also having to tell him to keep his hands in his pockets. He can't help himself, the silly sausage.

While they were there, I asked if either of them knew where I could get some brass section to fabricate the windscreen frame. Brett had put me onto someone in Victoria who had moulds to cast the brass windscreen standards. This was already under way. Fred informed me there was a place in Perth which dabbled in hard-to-get bits. "Woodsies Windscreens on Walter Road in Morley do that sort of thing. They carry new old stocks of rubber seals and stuff. Also do custom windscreens. Give the owner John a call Howie."

"Many thanks, I'll do that tomorrow. Then perhaps go down with some details."

After a while, Fred called a halt to the gum-flapping session, declaring that his wife Elaine was expecting him home for lunch with the family, so the two of them took off again, leaving me to make a mental note to contact Woodsies the next day, which was Monday.

Now, any of you 'car-smarts' out there familiar with the SS Jaguar will know that the windscreen is a work of art to say the least. The following Wednesday morning I was standing inside Woodsies Windscreens. The guy I was facing was only too familiar with the ornate SS windscreen.

"Ooh, one of those hey. We did a couple of them some years ago. Pretty fancy stuff," he offered, eyeballing me somewhat critically. "We carry the brass extrusions in stock. There are two – one for the baseline which is more than just a channel, and then the other is a plain 'C' channel."

This was happening. "Sounds good to me." I showed him some close-ups of Brett's car. "Is this the same as what you've got?"

"That's the one," he replied.

"Good. I'd like to get enough to cover the job please."

"Oh no, I'm sorry my friend – we don't sell the extrusion, we only supply the complete frames made to order." He informed me firmly.

"How come? Gee, I was hoping to do as much as possible myself. Can you make an exception?" I pleaded.

"Sorry, my boss John will never allow it. He paid big dollars to have the dies made at the mill and he needs to recoup his money," he explained.

"Well, I can understand that. But how about we do it this way?" I was thinking quickly. "Because it will be near impossible to match the shape of the scuttle for the base channel, it will have to be done on the car, and as it can't be brought all the way here from Northam, I suggest you sell me the base section, then I will form it into shape and bring it back here for you to cut and silver solder the 'C' channel uprights to it. But then I need to take it from there, as the top channel needs to be convex and I want to decide on the amount of curve only when the rest of the job is complete. I don't mind paying a bit extra to make up for some of what you lose by not doing the entire job," I added.

The guy knew what I suggested made sense and finally he agreed to go down that path. So I went home with a length of the base section on the back seat, feeling quite pleased with myself.

By this time the scuttle, complete with eyelids, was finished apart from final welding and perfecting a couple of points where the sheet metal had been joined, so I would be able to tackle this job immediately and get the windscreen frame behind me. Once the ornate rough cast windscreen standards arrived from Victoria, I would do all the necessary machining work to complete them, followed by fitting them and the frame. Then all that would be left was the glass to be cut. Good!

One morning, I was about to start work when my phone rang. It was Katz, the engineer. "Hello Howie, how are you?" he asked cheerfully (for a change).

"I'm good thanks. You got some news on those positions?"

"Yes," he told me, before adding, "but unfortunately you will have to find another engineer to continue. I'm moving to Queensland next month!"

'Shit' – I thought to myself. That can only spell problems. A new guy may not agree with some of the work that Katz had approved. Katz was really good. He was strict but always fair and wasn't full of his own importance albeit a bit abrupt at times. Katz told me where to position the cruciform members and the cross-member. I thanked him for his work and wished him well. 'Bugger.' Oh well, I'd ring around and talk to other engineers. But that was down the track. There was ample work to go on with that didn't require approval.

When I finally plucked up the courage to attempt a door, I decided to make a mock-up first without getting too fussy. Then I would go to Brett's place for comparison with his. He had given me some handy advice regarding a method he'd used to copy shapes. "A length of stick solder is soft and pliable," he'd said. I had rolled a piece around the radius on one of his doors and carefully brought it home so that it could be used on the mock-up. That worked a treat. The day I had taken the pattern of Brett's door, his Dad was visiting, and over a cup of tea I mentioned my intention was to build the doors prior to finalising the skeleton. My reasoning behind that was simple – it was easier to build the skeleton around the door rather than tamper with the shape and dimensions of a completed door. At first Brett had disagreed with this concept but soon saw sense in my line of thought when Dad (Ian) chimed in, declaring that he wished he'd thought of that at the time they built the doors for SS110.

Anyway, I turned good steel into shit a couple of times before producing something that seemed close enough to the mark. On an SS door, there are compound curves and I needed an English wheel, though I had not the slightest idea how to use one. And paying three thousand big ones for an English wheel was not an option. So, I converted my milling machine into one. First I unearthed a couple of old steel castors and machined them up. One went onto the head of the machine and the other into a mounting which was held in the vice. The up and down action on the table provided the pressure, and hey presto, an English wheel! And it worked too! Not very well, but good enough. Someone had lent me a video on the techniques, and after watching some guy performing magic, I proceeded to once again create scrap metal until I finally got the idea.

After making an arrangement to go back to Brett with the door, I went down and checked it out against his car. It wasn't far off and Brett looked at it from all angles, eventually declaring I was "getting there man" and that it "looked like an SS door". So, after having a careful look at the slight inevitable differences between the two doors, and recording everything with a black marker, I drove back to Northam. Now that I was on the right track with this particular part of the job, I made up my mind to spend the next four days on the doors – only the doors – and finish them completely.

At this point in time if a stranger walked into my workshop and saw the SS, they would have been forgiven for thinking it was at quite an advanced stage. Wrong. The thing was, that although there was a skeleton and the scuttle looked finished, it wasn't. The engine, gearbox and differential were propped up and held in place with temporary brackets and clamps. Northing was finished. No! I lie! The chassis was finished. It was by now fully welded and all the various mounting brackets etc. were in place other than the engine mountings which would be finalised after alignment. But walking around the car that afternoon after returning from Canning Vale, I felt that hollow, scared feeling again. There was no grill, no bonnet yet, no tub. And what about wheels? Where would I find wheels. '18" wires' that would fit a Volve hub! Headlights. Instruments. Wiring. I felt I was into something far bigger than I had first thought. The immensity of what still lay ahead hit me hard that day – like it would do many more times in the future.

Three pieces of 1mm cold rolled mild steel sheet pre-cut to the blank size ready for the doors lay against the wall behind the SS. On the way back from Brett's I had resolved to get started immediately upon my return. For a long moment I stood and gazed at the sheets, trying to psych myself into action. But I couldn't do it. I went to the fridge instead. And then the next day, the same thing happened. Something had gone wrong. I realised that the negative state of mind that was persisting here was probably the result of me over-reacting to the myriad challenges still ahead of me. I felt trapped. Deep down, I was certain of one thing – my pride would eventually win the battle and force me to keep going. Then I remembered somewhere in the mists of the past reading about 'Living in daylight compartments' by some psychologist in a Readers Digest article. Daylight compartments! That was it!

Gail had donated half a dozen old bed sheets and duvet covers to the workshop for my bikes. I dug them out, went over to the SS and covered it up. There! Sorted. All that was left was the mock-up door, and the sheet metal. From now on, there was no massive project ahead of me. Only lots of small ones. And who cares how long it takes. Not me. The next morning, I felt much better.

CHAPTER FOURTEEN

MOMENTARY LAPSE OF REASON The week following my loss of direction, things got really busy at work. A contract to make up a set of dies for mass producing cable hangers for the mines had come my way and that largely kept me away from the door. But I did keep the job going, albeit at a snail's pace. Normally, for someone with experience and confidence, the doors would be done simultaneously – operation by operation, a mirror image of the other. That way, one would have a better chance of the two being identical shapes. But I was decidedly lacking in both experience and confidence, and for that reason I tackled one at a time. Remember, the framework they were to fit into was not complete and even if the doors were not identical (which was on the cards), I had one important fact working in my favour. Nobody can look at both sides of the car at the same time. Sneaky hey!

So, all the while I was making dies, the partially made right-hand door was perched on a bench near me so I could eyeball it and contemplate my next move. Now it might sound like I am making a bigger deal of this than warranted, but I can assure you good readers, for me this was a very difficult task. If you don't know your stuff, the metal will demonstrate to your frustration just how unpredictable it can be.

But, do you know what? Every time you fuck something up – you learn. And learn I did. Again and again. Once the dies for the cable hangers were gone, I seized the opportunity to get back to the SS – No! the doors remember – not the SS.

And I worked and worked. For three or four days nobody turned up at my workshop and I buried myself in my task. Before long one door was finished. The right-hand one. It got a coat of primer and once it was dry enough to touch, I stood it on the bench propped up against the wall and grabbed a beer (*yes!* It was beer o'clock). Did I really do that? Excitement began to well up inside me. Then I carried it over to the car, pulled the covers off the right-hand side and offered it up. It looked just perfect, and for the first time in ages I felt proud of what I'd achieved. The reversing gearbox and the many other components I had designed were no big deal at all. I was trained to do things like that. But this was from another planet. This was the real deal. This was coach-building. My confidence was restored. I was back on BOOGIE STREET. I ripped into the left-hand door with gusto.

But soon, I would be taken down a peg or two again. In the excitement, I made a complete mess of the left-hand door. So, now you know why I cut three blanks! The enthusiastic amateur was back at work. The third try was good.

Peter Mawby was due in the following day for a cuppa, so I made the second door disappear with jet speed. ♫♫♫♪♪♫♪ Coward me! But I don't care.

The next stage was an interesting one and I was looking forward to tackling that job. It went something like this:

The SS, as everybody knows, has a long tapered snout. My big four-litre donk has a bulky aluminium plenum chamber – slung low down on the left-hand side. Well! That's okay, but wouldn't it just be my luck that the throttle body (which lives up at the front end) is positioned nicely so that the left-hand side of the bonnet, on its journey to the radiator cowl, collides with it to the tune of about fifty millimetres. This even after I had offset the engine to the right by thirty-five millimetres. And that had been the maximum offset, as had it been any more, the bell housing would have crept across and finished up cramping the area where the pedal box was to go.

But I knew that was coming earlier and had concocted a plan. First, off came the inlet manifold. Then, I simply cut the front end off just behind the bolt-on unit which houses the throttle butterfly (threaded holes and all). The same fate befell the rear section where a couple of vacuum hoses come from. And the two ends swapped places. Doing this helped but didn't quite get me there, so I took the manifold over to a friend who can make an aluminium welder talk and asked him to cut and 'v' the underside of the inlet passages so we could tuck the plenum chamber in enough to allow the bonnet to pass. So now, the air inlet was right down the back and dangerously close to the firewall – but it didn't matter. I had to feed the air through a flat custom made duct which would hold a pod type air filter. That worked well and it looked quite nice too, once it was installed.

Obviously, by now the differential was suspended in its final position, and that left the way open to do the all-important 'engine to differential alignment' – or should I say, vice-versa. My gut feeling is that these passages will no doubt be read by motor-heads like myself. Unlike some of you talented types out there, my non-existent knowledge of assembling a drivetrain and getting it right, put me on my guard, so before going ahead, I rang Peter Mawby. It was Friday afternoon.

"Hey Peter. When are you stopping in again?" I enquired.

"Good afternoon Howie. Funny you should ask. I need to do a service on the old man's Volvo and was going to ask you if I can bring it in. I have to come to the office for a spell in the morning. Are you working on the beast tomorrow?" he asked me.

"Sure am Peter, anytime. I'll be here till late."

"How about if I arrive about ten?" he ventured.

"That's fine with me. Also, I need to pick your brains on something."

"Sure thing. I'll see you then," he said, then signed off.

I was busy rummaging around among a number of old Volvo propshafts which I'd scored from Phil so I could fabricate one for the SS (dogs locked up this time).

Once we both had a cuppa in hand, I asked: "Peter, I'm about to begin aligning the engine and gearbox to the diff. Is there anything I need to know? We've only got one shot at this and I don't want to 'f' it up."

He laughed and walked over to the car. "Ah yes...is your diff in its final position Howie?" he asked.

"Yes, it's perfectly square to the chassis. I've made sure of that," I answered with some confidence – because I had made sure – very sure!

"So, how are you going to do it?" he asked, waving his hand at the gap where the prop-shaft would go, then continued: "Remember, it doesn't matter if the engine and gearbox unit is left or right of centre, or above or below, you only have to make sure that the centerline of the input shaft on the diff and the engine crankshaft are parallel lines. Also, for the record, although it won't apply here, as your engine is offset, it's really bad practice to align a gearbox and diff in a dead straight line or too close to it, because the uni-joints on the prop-shaft don't move. And in time, they tend to seize up," he concluded.

"Thanks Peter. That's some good advice as usual. What would I do without you!" I stated, grinning at him. "For the alignment, as far as the parallel lines thing is concerned, I'm going to make up two dummy shafts coming off the gearbox output shaft and the differential input shaft. If they are dead square, I can run them past each other and measure in-between to get it spot on," I told him.

Then he slapped me playfully on the shoulder. "You don't need me." He carried on with the Volvo.

While Peter was tinkering with his Dad's car, I found two flanges in the pile of prop-shaft components. One to suit the gearbox and one to suit the diff. I cut both the uni-joints and welded a suitable length of pipe onto the flanges as close to square as possible. Then, holding the pipe in the lathe chuck, I faced the flanges so that they would be true once bolted into position. So there was my aligning jig. All done and dusted – happy now.

Later that afternoon just before I went home, Harry materialised in the doorway.

"Harry Bloody Levenstein – how are you my friend?"

"Hello Boofhead. Are you staying out of trouble?"

"No!" I answered truthfully. "And you? What are you doing in my territory?"

He giggled. "On my way to Dowerin. Friend of mine has a Daimler

Dart he may want to sell. We've been talking about it for some time now. So I thought I might take a drive out and investigate. I'm having a week off."

Harry is a funny old bird. Two or three times a year he leaves his victims to a locum and goes mooching around the countryside without any particular destination. All on his own. Packs a bag and guitar and just drives. Stress relief. I like it. It was doubtful he would go for the Dart, as chronologically, the car is out of step with his taste. And also, Harry was not prone to untying his purse strings unless there was a good reason to do so. "So, you're still sniffing around hey," I said laughingly, then told him, "why don't you stop fucking around Harry and buy a Suffolk? That's what you really want. You know that."

"I'll see. I don't rush this kind of thing," he pointed out as he trudged across to the SS and, as usual, had a good look around, scrutinising the work done since his last visit, all the while pushing and pulling at things. Like Fred! Then he pointed to the empty void in front of the engine. "What are you doing about a radiator cowl," he enquired.

"Dunno yet. I'm not shelling our three grand – that's for sure!" I stated.

"There's a scrap metal dealer in Mundaring. I'm told he keeps some non-ferrous stuff. He may have some brass mesh," I commented as Harry began moving towards the door. "I may drop in and check it out."

Harry turned, and rubbing his chin thoughtfully, said: "Yes, yes, I'd forgotten about that place. My son was after something or other and we drove up there about five years ago. I recall the fellow's name was Roger – good sort – also building a car. It was an Allard. His place was packed with bits and pieces. Yes! Try him. You never know what he may have in there."

"Very interesting Harry!" I said, because it was. Then he was gone.

I decided that while Harry was away, I would push him over the edge. I would email Suffolk and enquire about the cost of landing one of their cars in Australia. I had a good idea what a fully built SS was worth in England, but import duties and the like would send the price north. I sent the same email twice but never got a reply. In the past, I had enquired about components and mentioned to them that I was building an SS, and wondered if perhaps they thought I was simply fishing for information.

Well I wasn't. In any event, as it turned out, Harry proved me wrong and the silly old sod bought the Dart. Then, soon after, he surprised us all and retired to New Zealand, Dart and all. I would miss him.

Soon after making my first cup of tea one morning, a lady walked in and introduced herself as Helen.

"I'm from the Avon Valley Advocate. Can I offer you some advertising? We have a special price at the moment." And she launched herself into the standard sales pitch which expounded the virtues of newspaper advertising etc., etc. – until I politely interrupted her and said:

"Thank you Helen, but I honestly don't have any use for advertising. I have more than enough work and I tend to keep my head down. I'm officially semi-retired, though if you look around, you wouldn't think so!"

"That's all good Howie. All good. Then she saw the partly built SS. "What have you got here?"

I told her.

"My boss loves old cars. Can I tell him about it?"

"Certainly! Tell him he's welcome to pop in and have a look – anytime!"

With that she shot through and I contemplated my next move.

It didn't take long. After lunch the same day, a distinguished looking gentleman, bald and bearded, broke into my thoughts as I was trying to solve a problem with a blanking die someone had asked me to fix, with a cheerful "Hello".

"Good afternoon."

"John Proud, Avon Valley Advocate," he said pointing at the car. "What have we here?"

I told him. "Oh My! This is going to be something I must follow," he exclaimed enthusiastically. "Would you mind if we did a feature on this from time to time? Northam doesn't see this kind of thing every day!"

"Yes, sure John," I told him. I took an immediate liking to the man.

"Howie, have you ever seen a Stutz Bearcat?"

"No!"

"Oh my goodness. Years ago I saw one at a show. It was stunning. I will dig out some pictures." And so, John Proud and myself gasbagged for the next half hour about cars before he suddenly looked at his watch.

"Must be off. But I'll be back," he stated and went away to do whatever newshounds do.

Over the years, John came back religiously to take photos, ask questions and sometimes just to chat. The car was featured in the local paper several times during the build. A kind of progress report. Magic!

CHAPTER FIFTEEN

RODNEY GETS THE WHEELS TURNING It was winter 2009, and by now my windscreen minus the glass was all finished and fitted. The plan with Woodsies had gone well, and so had all the machining work and fitting. Great fun. The drive-train was complete and I now turned my attention to a problem which had been gently gnawing away at my subconscious for years but was now looming large. Wheels. Fucking eighteen-inch wheels! Wires! Bolt on, to take narrow cross-ply tyres and to suit a 1970s Volvo hub. A big ask – what was I thinking?

"According to a friend of mine Boofhead, there's a fellow in Wangara who spends his days working on English cars – Rovers, Jags, Austins and everything else apparently." This was Harry ringing from New Zealand to chat to me while I was travelling back from Wongan Hills with Gail, who at one time had a job up there. I had decided to tag along with her and check out the local wreckers. We were ready to go when Gail's phone rang and she got into a conversation with one of her work colleagues about netball. From what I could make out, the girl was quite a gun in the local league. I overheard Gail congratulating her for winning some game or other.

"How come you didn't tell her about your netball career?" I asked after she had rung off,

"Oh, I didn't want to do that. She is quite excited about how she is going," she answered with a grin.

So modest my dear lady. The truth is that in her young years Gail had represented Natal Province in South Africa at netball. She was also an accomplished surfer and took part in competitions at beaches around Durban, in the company of the likes of Shaun Thompson and his brother Mark, among other big names in the surfing community.

Anyway, back to Wongan Hills – I got her to drop me off at the local wrecker, who from a distance, seemed to have a lot of old stuff down the back. He did have a lot of stuff down the back – a shitload in fact – but nothing I could use. Pietersie was searching for gold in a city street as usual. Gail pulled into the Goomalling BP for fuel and two of their delicious toasted bacon and egg sandwiches.

"Do you know what he calls himself?" I had asked Harry when he had told me about the guy in Wangara.

"No, but it's in the new section. Sniff it out. May be a good call – you never know," Harry had concluded

The guys at Stegbar had left a message on my phone asking me to pull in there and check on one of their dies. I made a mental note to seek out the place Harry had spoken about.

The following week I went to Wangara and found the place almost immediately, though it wasn't in the new section. Outside, awaiting attention, was a half done 1961 Austin Westminster, graced on either side by a pair of early Mini sedans (both in pristine condition). I spent a few minutes drooling over the Minis and indulging in some nostalgia peering into the Austin. Nostalgia being the key word as the 61 Westminster had been my first car.

I ambled across the yard to the workshop and presented myself conspicuously beneath the roller door. Two workers were busy doing what these guys do best – making a noise. A man wearing faded green overalls spied me out of the corner of his eye and detached himself from what appeared to be a rocker cover from an old Cortina or Anglia. Picking up a rag and wiping his hands, he walked over to me, looking a little unhappy.

"How can I help?" he asked grudgingly.

"Sorry to intrude!"

"It's okay but we are busy at the moment. What are you looking for?" He seemed to be irritated for some reason. Maybe the rocker cover hadn't been co-operating and had given him the shits.

"It's a long shot I know, but I'm looking for some 18" wires and some headlights that would suit an SS Jaguar."

"You got an SS Jaguar?" It sounded more like an accusation than a question.

"No! Actually, I'm building one," I replied.

"Forget it pal, there are no free lunches with shit like that. You'll have to buy replica bits like the rest of us," he told me then treated me to a mocking chuckle and continued, gesturing to the two 1930s Rover saloons parked up against the rear wall. "I built those two. Just had to get all the bits in from England."

"Fair enough," I said. The guy had a bad attitude. What does it take to be polite for crying out loud.

"What's this SS you're working on anyway? What chassis?"

"I built the chassis in my workshop …."

He wouldn't let me finish. "Do you realise they won't let you license it!" he announced conclusively.

Here we go again I thought. History repeating itself. I had enough of this rude idiot. I was about to say 'Thanks for nothing' to the guy, when a remote bell from the office telephone dragged him away. I immediately took the gap and walked towards my car as this negative character disappeared through a doorway into an office.

During my encounter, I couldn't help noticing one of the nearby workers secretly taking an interest in the proceedings. Before I had taken four steps he dropped what he was doing and quickly glided across to me, flashing a glance towards the office door. He had a strong London East End accent. "Don't worry about him mate, he's a fucking rude bastard. Doesn't even own the place. If I were you, I would be ringing up when Jack is in and complain. He does this all the time!"

I simply said thank you to the man and left. The incident in Wangara made me feel unhappy during my journey home that day. So far, in my quest to collect parts for the SS project, everybody had been so helpful and encouraging. Well…such is life!

So, we began searching the internet. I say 'we' because at the time, I was about as computer literate as a Nile crocodile and Gail had to help me press the buttons. I almost drove her batty looking for those wheels, believe me. Eventually, we unearthed a British company that distributed wires and mags for an Indian factory. Some really beautiful chrome wires came up on their website, and we pored over the many styles and dimensions available. I was in the next room when suddenly Gail let out a yelp of excitement and declared that she'd found something. And so she had. An 18" Wire, 72 spoke with identical hold pattern, made to fit the 'X' Type Jaguar around year 2000. Bingo! Only drawback was, they were 8" wide. But that wasn't the end of the world. I would contact them and check out the possibility of having some specially made that were 5.5" wide.

Excited now!

So we sent off some emails. First to the agent in England – who dismissed my idea out of hand – followed by one to the factory in India, who were not quite as blunt but indicated that the price to set up for five wheels of an un-standard width, would resemble a telephone number. As it was, the agent in England had quoted me £375.00 each. That's before tyres and tubes! Bugger.

Unhappy now! But all avenues by this time had been exhausted and we resigned ourselves to the fact that purchasing them from England was our only option. I would split the rims on the lathe, remove a section, and have them robot welded. It was going to be expensive. A friend of mine had bought his wife an X-Type Jaguar some years before, and I rang him.

"Rodney Wright," came a familiar gruff voice down the line.

"Hello Rodney. Long time no speak," I said cheerfully.

"I recognise the voice but I can't remember the face," he said jokingly.

"Yeah, It's been a while," I said. "We need to catch up more often Rodney! I need a favour. Have you still got your Jaguar?"

"Yes!"

I explained the situation and asked him to be kind enough to check the dimensions on their spare wheel, just to make certain that the wheels in England would be correct. He did that and rang back to confirm.

"Yes. The spare matches the dimensions you gave me. Before you go ordering wheels, why not have a chat with Tony at Roadbend Jaguar. He may have some there."

"That's a long shot Rodney. Surely those wheels wouldn't be a stock item?" I ventured.

"We don't know that. Leave it with me. Don't do anything," he said firmly and rang off.

Half an hour later, an amazing turn of events: "Go down to Roadbend and see Tony. He's got four of those wheels for you. Twelve hundred dollars for the lot. Used, but near new."

"Good God. Where did they come from?"

"A stroke of luck. A customer had ordered them in and had them fitted but after a while the air started leaking past the spoke nipples according to Tony, and the customer asked for his old wheels to be re-fitted. So the guy wants to sell them. Be quick!"

And so, I marked myself present at Roadbend Jaguar on the same day and picked my wheels up. And to top it all, Tony gave me a lovely book on the SS Jaguar which had been standing on their shelf amongst some manuals. I was over the moon.

On the way home, I decided to pay the scrap metal guy in Mundaring a visit, which was only a minute or so off Great Eastern Highway. Walking into the building, two things caught my eye simultaneously – directly in front of me stood the Allard Harry had mentioned – very nearly complete from where I was standing. There was nobody around. Also from where I was standing, thirty degrees to my right and hung high on a wall, the un-mistakable shape of a dust covered Jaguar MK V radiator cowl (albeit incomplete). I was quivering with excitement when a man came out of an office door below where the radiator cowl was hanging. He turned out to be Roger, the owner. An absolute gentleman. Very car savvy and interesting. After I explained what mischief I was up to, he showed me his collection of cars which included a fabulous Austin Healy 3000. Also, a pretty little Fiat 124 Sport.

We chatted for a while and I finally said: "Roger, the reason I came here was to see if you had any of the diamond woven mesh in brass for my radiator cowl and grill, but I couldn't help noticing that old Mark Five cowl you have hanging outside your office." I stated hopefully. "Is that for sale?"

Roger wouldn't take any money for the cowl and simply said: "You take it. That can be my contribution to your very interesting project."

I thanked him profusely and headed home. It had proved to be a big day for my project.

A Mark V radiator cowl is about four inches wider than the SS100, but virtually the same shape. What I had acquired from Roger provided me with the all-important top and the two sides, but they needed to be extended and a lower section fabricated. So, on face value, the job meant a cut and sheet off the top section, and for the bottom end, a bit of brass sheet and a few persuasive blows would give me a dimensionally correct cowl to work with. That would allow work to begin on a suitable radiator. Up to now, I hadn't been able to continue with the radiator, but once the cowl was done, the job could go ahead. The intention was to squeeze the biggest, thickest, most efficient core possible in, to cope with the extreme temperatures we in the West Australian Wheatbelt, experience. I would pick up an old radiator from a truck or the like from Northam Radiators and cut it to size, then once I'd decided exactly where the entry and exit fittings were to be located, knock up a dummy for them to replicate.

Then, a minor setback! The rims were too large to fit into my lathe. Fortunately, the firm that did the welding offered to do them at a good price. The day I transported my rims to Kalamunda, I pulled into a bottle shop on the way and bought a bottle of Dimple Haig Whiskey, had it gift wrapped and went and dropped it off in Mundaring for Roger. While I was there, I bought a small sheet of brass from him to see me right with the radiator cowl, then with a promise to drop in again, I headed for Kalamunda. One the way home I detoured and drove up to Rodney Wright's house in Lakelands. On the way, I shot into another bottle shop and came out with a cold carton of his favourite beer. I pulled into his shed and dropped the carton onto his bench. He had his head buried under the dash of his little Triumph TR3A he'd been restoring.

"Many thanks for fixing me up with those wheels," I said.

He pointed to the beers. "You didn't need to do that."

I waved him away. "How lucky was that. You must have known Tony had them," I told him with a grin.

"Absolutely not! I hadn't spoken to Tony for months. When I followed up, he told me those four he sold you were the only set they had supplied. Pure luck!" he declared, then said: "Come here, I've got something else for you!"

I followed him over to a shelving unit packed with motorbike engines and ancillaries. Presently, after digging around in a metal cabinet, he produced a small package wrapped in a plastic bag, secured by a rubber band. He plopped it into my hand.

"Open it!' he instructed.

"What's this?"

'A present. Just open it!" he barked impatiently.

I removed the plastic and opened the box. Inside, a splendid pair of chrome plated vintage Lucas torpedo park lights. How about that!

"Wow! Thank you Rodney," I said. "These are something else that won't have to be sourced now."

"After we rang off the other day, I remembered them. Picked them up at a swap meet in case I needed to replace the ones on the Rolls, but I can't see me ever needing them, so they are yours." Then, after declaring that the working day was now over, he extracted two beers and I followed him to his favourite spot in the garden where a group of magpies were perched on an outdoor setting table

The Rolls Rodney had referred to was a 1932 20-25. The 'Wright Toy Box' also contained an enviable motorcycle collection. Add to that, a Triumph Stagg, MGB and an un-restored road registered 1927 Dodge.

As we approached the garden set, the magpies took off, but once we settled into a chair, they all returned and Rodney began feeding them bits of minced meat from a container he'd taken from his workshop fridge. The birds were all over the table and even perched on Rodney's shoulder. We sipped our beers and exchanged news for a while until the sun dipped below the tree line and it began to get cold. It was time to get back to my lady. I thanked my friend once again for his help and went away.

CHAPTER SIXTEEN

WAR MUSEUM Back in the mists of the past, the reader will recall Frank, the technician from Valley Ford, had me make up some parts for the military vehicle he was building. Over the years I had become well acquainted with Frank. One time, he invited me to his house/home workshop – actually to see if I could help him with a problem that had developed with his now (almost complete) armoured car. While I was there, I asked him how his interest in German military vehicles had come about. He laughed and answered with a smile.

"I honestly couldn't tell you Howie. Maybe from reading about war machinery in general, but the German stuff was good," before adding, "have I showed you my collection!?"

"No, have you got more stuff than this?" I waved a hand to gesture at an open carport housing the armoured car, a Second World War Mercedes truck and BMW motorcycle with sidecar, all adorned with the appropriate livery.

"Come inside," he beckoned and I followed. Frank, at the time, lived in an average sized three-bedroom house in average Northam suburbia. I remember going inside and glancing casually around before he led me through a doorway and down a couple of steps. He closed the door behind me. Here, a jaw dropping spectacle confronted me. So help me, I found myself standing in a fucking German war museum, no less. Genuinely taken aback, I uttered incredulously:

"Frank! I had no idea. Good God, where did you pick all this stuff up from?"

"Oh, all over the world Howie. I bid for stuff on the internet. I check the newspaper adds. Just a hobby mate," he explained as we walked past life-size mannequins in full Gestapo and SS uniforms. I was gob smacked and barely heard him say: "Like this cap for instance." He mentioned something about some prominent German regiment. "I bid for this one and was chuffed when I got it. Two thousand dollars only. From America. I wonder if I'll get my money back one day. Do you reckon I will?" he laughed.

I laughed too. "I reckon you will Frank. I reckon you will." Never a dull moment! Fuck!

Sorry, I'm getting off the point but I just had to tell you about that. So, fast forward back to the present. It was time to get something done about the electrics on the SS and Frank was my man. So I pulled him in to discuss things and check out the gear that Lee (the Wrecker guy in Bayswater) had supplied. It was all piled into a large box in a corner of the workshop, and I hauled it into view so that Frank had access to it. It was a Friday afternoon when Frank turned up on his motorbike to assess the wiring job. Only minutes before, I'd reacted to a whimpering coming from the fridge and he joined me as we laid the contents of the box on the floor. What a mess. Frank sorted through everything, making mental notes and uttering the terminology of various components, while I crouched alongside him trying hard to look intelligent, though I had no idea what we were looking at.

Finally he stood up and said with a satisfied smile: "All seems to be here, except the carbon canister. Did he give you one?"

"I wouldn't know what a carbon canister was if I was pissing on one Frank," I told him truthfully. "What does that do?"

"It's an emission control thing. You'll need it for licensing," he explained.

"Maybe that guy in Bayswater forgot. I'll have a yarn with him Frank."

Much modification needed to be done to the wiring harness, as apart from it being too long overall, a number of functions had to be deleted, such as heater, demister, air-conditioning, cruise control and all manner of other things Frank had listed. I gave him a key for the workshop so that he could come and go whenever he felt inclined to do some work. So, there was another job I could put aside. Goodo!

I had been itching to start work on the bonnet, and had resolved to try as hard as I could to produce an excellent looking job, since the bonnets on these cars were a focal point and the level of quality here could spell a major plus or minus, aesthetically. Construction of this item was going to be a protracted and complex affair (for me at any rate), and I was terrified. One mistake on the louvers and an entire panel would finish up in the bin – and all four sections of the bonnet needed to be completely formed up prior to punching the louvers. Being a toolmaker, I'd made a considerable number of louver dies for electrical panels and the like so that part didn't scare me. But what did scare me was that my hand-operated Heine press was all I had to work with and its tonnage was not up to the job. It was capable of forming the louvers, but not slitting the material and forming in one operation. So, I grew a brain – or so I thought.

My reasoning was that if I cut all the slits with an angle grinder, using a narrow cutting wheel, it would only be a matter of forming the louvers in my fly press. If I made jigs to contain the cut lengths, an entire row of slits could be achieved, and then I would simply form the louvers up in the dies – Easy. Ironstein, me!

So I spent a couple of days feverishly knocking up the forming dies. As all of you SS heads out there know, there are three different sets of louvers. Two lots on the bonnet sides and the short ones on top – millions of them. Once the dies were complete, I found a stray piece of one millimeter mild steel sheet and proceeded to cut a series of slits as per my plan. I then cleaned up the burrs and bravely went over to the press where the first forming die was set up. What happened next took me by surprise. Unwittingly, by pre-cutting a row of slits, I had shot myself in the foot. When louver number one was formed, because of the slit for the next one was already there, the forming action lifted the material behind it and deformed it at the ends, before again being flattened as the die bottomed out. My plan was falling apart. Bugger!

If I'd had a more powerful press the dies could have been made to cut and form the material simultaneously as per standard procedure, and I wouldn't have landed up in this mess.

So with a heavy heart, I capitulated and rang up an old acquaintance in Perth, Anton, a toolmaker like myself and asked him to punch the bonnet louvers for me. I kept the antics of the preceding twelve hours to myself. Anton's company had a dazzling array of louver dies, amassed over the years from punching bonnets for the street rod community, and others. After flicking him a photo of the Boughton bonnet along with some dimensions, he returned with a quote of $500. The cost of building a vehicle such as the one in progress here can become scary, and every cent laid out on outside work, adds to the big picture. So, disappointed as I was about having to employ Anton to do the bonnet, I realised that $500 amounted to petty cash compared to what it would have cost had I converted my time into dollars. Common sense must prevail.

With mixed feelings, I dragged out a nice shiny sheet of one millimeter cold rolled steel and attacked it. The hinge arrangement on top of the original SS bonnet was a bit of a complex affair as far as I could remember because a chrome plated hinge needed to be connected to a would-be painted surface. I decided that because the intention was to do a 'fold and flatten' operation on the edge of the material that the hinge connected to, the thickness doubled up and I could simply MIG weld the hinge to the bonnet through every third hole, after chrome plating, then simply mask the hinge prior to painting the panels. Overall, the bonnet actually turned out to be pretty straightforward (even for me), apart from one or two stages such as rolling the top sections, which up at the scuttle end, had a considerably larger radius than down at the radiator end.

And so it all came together, much to my delight. Anton did a great job of the louvers and my dies finished up gathering dust on a shelf, unused.

Late one Sunday afternoon after extricating myself from the couch, I felt the urge to do some design work on the headlights. Somewhere in the mists of the past, I'd had a quote for two replica units from England for the princely sum of four thousand Australian dollars, which I'd dismissed immediately, vowing, as usual, to 'find a way'. Back in the day, the SS was available with either the standard 10.25" lights, which were perfectly proportioned to the vehicle or the lovely looking Lucas P100s, which were a whopping 12" in diameter. I had seen photos, and in my opinion these lights became too much of a focal point and the overall picture was somewhat unbalanced. I had to shoot over to the workshop to pick up some close-ups of Brett's headlights and an old P100 someone had loaned me declaring I should consider P100s as they were readily available. I had graciously accepted the light on loan because I liked the idea of copying the ornate hinge arrangement.

So, pulling up outside the workshop in Gail's Mini, I entered through the side door and once inside, strode toward my 'office'. As I opened the bottom drawer of my desk to retrieve the photos, a voice stopped me in my tracks and made my blood curdle.

"Howie! How are you?"

I whipped around to see where the voice had come from. Now, I could have uttered something like: "Oh hello Frank, my goodness, you startled me." But that never happened.

"Fuck Frank! I just about crapped myself," I blurted.

"Sorry. I'd forgotten I'd brought my bike inside. Shit! You wouldn't have known," he returned, now beginning to grin. I grinned too now and then I just started to laugh – partly because of what had just happened and partly because of the spectacle in front of me.

Frank was sitting on a chair between the car and the wall with a battery operated reading light strapped to his forehead. Straddling his lap, was the wiring harness, or what was left of it. A large hard-covered manual was perched upright on a chair opposite him so he could consult it without moving. And there was wire everywhere. It looked like disorganised chaos. But I knew it wasn't. I pulled up another chair.

"Thank God it's you doing this Frank and not me."

CHAPTER SEVENTEEN

ENTER THE TITANIC So, okay. Frank continued practicing his black art, while I returned home armed with the P100 and photos. These I arranged on an occasional table in the lounge room and sat back on a dining chair with the SS book gifted to me by the Jaguar shop. A look of distaste didn't go unnoticed when the boss walked into the room and settled in a nearby recliner to watch some TV. She hadn't forgotten that memorable occasion when she'd arrived home and caught me red-handed polishing my motorbike in the kitchen, and ever since had kept a tight rein on my indoor activities.

"Have you given her a name yet? You know she has to have one," Gail enquired, interrupting my thoughts.

"Not yet, I've had a few ideas though, but it hasn't come to me. I suggested 'bug eyes' to Rodney and he was disgusted," I told her.

"Bug eyes! No. That name is used for the little Austin Healy Sprite. Your SS is a glamorous car. Think of something else – not 'bug eyes'," he had boomed over the phone.

"Something to do with all those curves maybe," Gail offered. "Curvy something or other."

And that was the trigger. Like a bolt of brilliance it struck me. I'd seen a snatch on TV about the movie *Titanic* and the very tasteful nude scene when Leonardo Di Caprio does a pencil portrait of Kate Winslet lying on a couch. The presenter had referred to her as 'Curvy Kate' Winslet. Curves. 'Curvy Kate!' It just sounded perfect. And she would wear it well.

Back to the lights – again. Now, holding the P100 upright and the right way up, I noted the exquisitely formed hinge was on the underside and the knurled knot for closing the rim was at the top. It was a case of beauty and the beast. Why hide the ornamental aspect underneath? I asked myself. I made up my mind there and then to copy the P100. Only, I would downsize them to 10.25" and turn them upside down. Excited now, I wanted to press buttons and pull levers. The plan was to metal spin the bodies from copper sheet, then, to cut a very long story short, make up a chrome-plated bezel that fitted behind the mesh and glass. This bezel would hold a large modern sealed beam lamp which would conform to the legal requirements the finished light needed to meet.

And then there were the taillights. Unorthodox to say the least. "They resemble an owl's face," someone, I forgot who, had offered – it may have been in the Jag book. So now that's what I call them, owl lights. But how would I make them? Once again, the Boughtons had provided me with a start on this one when I'd approached them.

"We finished up finding an original pair in the US. But let me check with Brett. When we were sniffing around, a guy gave us a couple of bits made from fiberglass. If they haven't been binned you're welcome to them Howie," Ian said, then added: "By the way, when you're looking for running board tread, come down here. I'm tripping over the stuff."

Peter Mawby was standing alongside me at the workbench and we were eyeballing the two items.

"I wonder why they're made from fiberglass Peter!"

"No doubt, some prick has taken the easy way out I'd say, and made replicas from fiberglass – remember, you can get plastic chromed these days," he commented.

And he was probably right, I thought. For a long time after Peter had gone, I studied the bits. For a start, the body, as the reader will no doubt agree, if made from metal, either required a deep drawing die or a complex fabrication job. The front piece that housed the lenses was full of imperfections, but otherwise, looked correct. How could I make this thing? I carried on with something else and pondered the problem for the rest of the day.

The answer came on the way home. So I turned around and went back. On my paint shelf, stood a can of fiberglass filler. I mixed a batch and filled the hollow front cover and neatly leveled it off. Now I was ready to perform an old toolmakers' trick. It had to wait until the next day when the fiberglass was fully set. After a restless night, I was back in the workshop at sparrow's fart and got straight back into it.

Fortunately, the copper for my headlights was already in. After cutting a piece large enough to cover the solid mould I'd made, I double annealed the copper. Next, I placed the mould in my fly-press and positioned the copper sheet over it. I then cut up some 16mm thick rubber sheet into five pieces that overhung the copper sheet by about 20mm. These, stacked one on top of another, gave me a solid rubber block about 80mm high. I positioned them on top of the copper sheet. Then after placing a solid piece of mild steel plate on the copper blank, I brought the press down as hard as I could. Like magic I was presented with a near perfect facsimile of my fiberglass mould.

And dear reader, if that display of brilliance didn't impress you, how about this? Instead of playing Einstein and attempting to form the bodies from copper, I decided to play left field. I made from solid jarrah. Yeah! Yeah! I hear you out there. Cop out! Cop out! Well go ahead and laugh. See if I care. Hee-hee!

To be sure the construction of the taillights conformed to current Australian design rules I rang Katz, who was, as mentioned earlier, now living on the eastern seaboard.

"As long as you use lenses and internal electrics that carry the appropriate ADR compliance, you can do what you like, as long as they don't fall to pieces," he informed me. "And how is the beast getting along anyway?" A faint chuckle drifted down the line.

"So far, so good. I'll send you some pictures – listen, I haven't chased up another engineer yet. Can't you carry on with the job remote?" I asked him, and after a long contemplation he agreed to inspect the progress via emails etc. This was a plus for me as Katz had some confidence in my work and knew I would stick to the rules. If, at the end of the journey, it became necessary for him to attend, I would pick up the tab for an airfare. Good.

In the meantime, Frank finished doing the wiring thing in return for machining work, and I had a ball building the lights and mountings etc. The reader will note from images, that some considerable changes were made in this area.

Throughout the creation of 'Curvy Kate', when it came to simplifying things without affecting the big picture, I confess I did give myself some slack but was happy with the changes made to the headlight supports, along with all the other components that weren't exactly as per the original.

By this time, the car looked as if it was almost finished apart from seals, interior trim and finishings, but a trained eye peeping under the dash would reveal the absence of wiring to the instruments and the windscreen wiper mechanism, which I'd yet to design and construct. The sobering truth that the end was still way below the horizon, didn't stop the little boy in me standing back and marveling at the spectacle. Did I really build this thing? Little old me?

But now was the time to be extra vigilant and avoid doing anything that may create a problem with licensing. Katz had warned me that his job was largely to do with the structural integrity of the vehicle, and small details relating to the final test by Licensing were up to me to get right. And speaking of licensing, a thousand years ago I had visited Alec, the kind gentleman who had provided some coaching on how to build a door. He had shown me around the replica 1928 Mercedes Benz he had been busy building. I remember asking the old man whether he intended licensing the car.

"I hope so. But I haven't got an engineer yet. Maybe I'll leave it until I'm finished. So, you think it will be alright?" he had asked.

"It should be," I lied. "But maybe get someone to have a look. I don't know enough about the technicalities," I continued, telling another lie in the same sentence. Truth be known, I'd been invited to have a look underneath, and even at the early stage of my journey, one look had told me that he was going to have to make some serious changes to satisfy the requirements of an ICV (individually constructed vehicle). The engine was from a 1971 Mercedes 230 six and was too old to conform. But the car looked good and I wasn't about to comment on these obvious issues Alec would need to address, so I gave the subject a wide berth.

Moral of the story – please, if any of you out there decides to tackle an ICV, do your homework and register your project with Transport!

CHAPTER EIGHTEEN

GEOMETRY REVISITED It was the other side of Christmas 2011 and Northam was blazing hot as I sat on a milk crate in my workshop, contemplating my next move.

Allan from Allan's Auto Electrics had wired up my dashboard instruments and I had concocted a wiper mechanism – albeit bizarre in appearance – that worked quite well. Most of the car was now complete and I had employed a local engineer to continue with the final bits and pieces. Katz was finally satisfied with the car and had, to my great relief, signed it off. This left the interior trim, seats and above all, the seatbelts.

It is common knowledge among vintage car nuts, that early vehicles had no seatbelts, and to this day they don't need them – even if the vehicle is entirely rebuilt. But Curvy Kate presented a problem. An ICV must have them. Any modern roadster has an ugly looking contraption up behind the seats that houses the seatbelt straps. This has to do with the geometry required to transfer loads back to the chassis. How could I introduce such an abomination on an SS? It wasn't going to happen!

How many nights I slept on the seatbelt problem is anybody's guess but I made up my mind to find a way to design something that would be unobtrusive and yet still meet the requirements. So I resolved to keep sleeping on it and carry on with the seats.

This was yet another headache, as the seats were required to be fitted with sliders for adjustment. And guess what? I hunted around the wreckers for something suitable, but every seat I looked at had a negative, one way or another. Either too wide or too high. Inside a storeroom at the rear of the old hotel, was a collection of odds and ends left over from my love affair with Minis. Among them were a couple of seats from an early Clubman. They were also too wide. I decided to revert to skullduggery. Fuck the consequences. A cunning plan was forming. The seats would need re-foaming and reupholstering, so first, off came everything.

As a result of the engine being offset to the right, the width between the tunnel and door had lost 35mm on the driver's side and gained as much on the passenger side, so basically, I could take advantage of this and make the passenger side more roomy. Now that I'd decided to break the rules, the world was at my feet. And my plan was now in sharp focus. First, cut and shut the Mini seats to the width and then I would source a set of front seats from any modern small car, cut the sliders out and fit them to the Mini seats.

Once I'd finished the job, it looked robust and my conscience got the better of me, so I pulled the engineer in to check them out. He was happy with the integrity and I had them upholstered. Job done. Happy again!

Rodney Style was my new engineer. When he came to check out the seats, I threw the seatbelt problem at him. The main stumbling block here is the downward angle off the horizontal the strap takes from the shoulder to the anchor point. I forget the precise figure but if the slope exceeds the required maximum, the argument quite rightly is that in the event of an accident, the downward forces that come into play when the upper torso is thrust forward, would likely crush your shoulder blade. So, one inescapable fact was that a bar of some sort would have to be constructed somewhere behind the seats for the belt to come from. The question was, how high did it have to be? I dropped one of the newly upholstered seats into position and sat inside. Rod Style was leaning up against the workbench watching me with interest.

"See, Rod. My shoulder is way above the level of the tub."

"How tall are you?" he asked.

"About five foot eleven."

"Is your seat adjusted fully forward?"

"No."

"Well, move it forward!"

"Ah! I know what you're getting at."

"Yes, and not everybody is as tall as you. So let's do some measurements," he said bringing a tape measure over.

"What are your intentions behind here?" he asked, indicating the empty space between the back of the seats and the rear of the tub.

"Just a small luggage space, that's all Rod."

"Okay then. Let's see. If a person, say three inches shorter than you was in that seat, then with the seat fully forward, the angle will just about make it, if the anchor point is at the level of the tub behind your door. But that will only give you about a foot or so for luggage. A bit more maybe," he said with a wicked grin.

"That would be just fine Rod. That gives me something to work on. Many thanks for your help."

I paid him for the visit and he went away. It was good to be working with somebody with a bit of imagination. He had solved my problem. All I had to do now was design something reasonably ornate to act as both a barrier to the small luggage space and a seatbelt mounting. Progress today!

Actually, it got better. My images will show that the inertia reels are not visible. That is because I managed to grow a brain once again and ordered the belts considerably longer than standard. I then mounted the inertia reels on top of a plate that houses the rear coil spring and fed the belt through a series of direction changes, until it came through a support positioned nicely at the top of the tub behind the doors.

During the engineer's visit, he had brought my attention to a number of interesting requirements relating to licensing. One of them was an immobiliser. Now, normally this wouldn't have presented a problem, except that when Frank had thinned out my wiring harness, he had removed some of the systems that were superfluous. For example, Curvy Kate had no use for air-conditioning, power steering, temperature and pressure warning system and many other modern functions. I had told him all that was needed was engine management and an ignition switch. And that's what I got. So, no immobiliser.

"What should I do Rod?" I asked the engineer.

"The requirement is that when the ignition key is removed, the vehicle cannot be driven," he answered with an impish smile. "Think about it."

I did think about it. All bloody night. Next day I had Rod Style on the phone.

"How about if I fitted a steering lock? A manual one with a key?" I asked hopefully.

He thought about it for a while and then asked: "What type of lock were you thinking of?"

I could fit a bracket onto the steering column with a hole in it, and then fit a dead lock like the ones they use on sliding doors," I offered, to which he replied:

"That sounds okay," then added: "Just make sure it's solid."

So I spent a few hours building the locking arrangement that afternoon. It was pretty straightforward and worked well. I was pleased

But I wasn't ready for what happened next. The phone rang. It was Style.

"That idea won't work!" he announced.

"Why not? I've done it already and it works fine," I said, surprised.

"Sorry, at the time we were a little hasty. If you lock the steering and jump into the car to drive you may forget about it, and that could be dangerous. We'll have to devise something else," he explained. And it was true, very true.

Bugger! Again.

Oh well, I would, as usual, eventually come up with something. It was beer time and I cracked one. It suddenly occurred to me that if I was able to somehow lock the handbrake on, the safety issue would go away.

My handbrake arrangement was custom made using basic components from the Volvo donor car. It was quite accessible from underneath and I jacked the car up to have a look. Alongside the ratchet housing, there was ample room to mount a small solenoid. If I pulled the handbrake up and then drilled a hole right through both the housing and ratchet plate, the solenoid shaft could be made to enter the hold and lock the handbrake on. This, under the solenoid's spring tension. By connecting the power for the solenoid to the ignition switch, it would retract from the brake once turned on, and allow the brake to be released. When the ignition switch was turned off and the brake pulled up, it would lock again. Bingo!

Style was tickled with this and immediately gave me the green light. Even the enthusiastic amateur is not immune from tiny flashes of brilliance. Tee-hee!

The most idiotic regulation for licensing ever to be legislated, was the sun reflection on chrome plating. Talk about the pen being mightier than the sword! When Style had announced that the rear of my beautiful chrome plated headlights needed to be blackened out, I was astounded.

"What utter horseshit," I had blurted.

He had thrown his hands up helplessly and said: "Rules are rules. No matter how silly they may seem! And that isn't all! All chrome in line of sight from the driver's seat, needs to be blacked out. Even those chrome bezels around your instruments."

"What about the windscreen surround? The whole effing thing is chrome Rod." I ranted on, the pressure beginning to take its toll on me. If I'd listened to McGrath, none of this would be happening. An old chassis with original numbers could have seen this project done as a restoration and exempt from a whole range of additions I'd been forced into.

Even my tiny little doors had not escaped the wrath of the pen. Side intrusion bars had to be welded in. The list goes on. But, enough of that! I would think of something.

CHAPTER NINETEEN

IGNITION Winter of 2013. 'Curvy Kate' was finally finished, apart from paint and one or two finishings.

After much agonising about the chrome reflection fiasco, I decided to simply do nothing about it and adopt a 'wait and see attitude' until Style came for his final inspection.

One afternoon I marked myself present at Licensing in Northam on a matter unrelated to the car, and thought I might investigate some personalised plates – which were an inescapable subject here. Under no illusions about my chances of getting something close to 'SS100', I asked the lady to check if 'SS100H' was available. The Boughtons had come close at 'SS110'. So I assessed my chances of getting 'SS100H' as about the square root of FA – but it cost nothing to ask. You can imagine my surprise when the lady told me it was available. No prizes for guessing how long it took me to fill in the application.

It was July the 21st, 2013 – precisely eight years since my friction saw had attacked the very first piece of RHS that would become the chassis. A small group of people were gathered in my workshop. It was 7.30pm and freezing cold.

Gail, our son Robin, Frank and I stood around Curvy Kate, ready. The big moment had arrived. Gail had her iPad set to video and Robin sat behind the wheel. Robin is a toolmaker by trade. From a tender age, he developed an uncanny ability to understand all things mechanical. By the time he turned 22 Robin was able to design and build both press tools and plastic injection moulds, was fully conversant with CNC production machines and computer aided design of engineering components. Not unlike Peter Mawby, Robin, on the occasions when he'd come home to visit for a few days, had participated in several brainstorming sessions over a couple of beers. It's great to have another engineering brain in the family.

There was still a lingering doubt in my mind about the possible computer problem pointed out by Lee, the guy who had sold me the engine. Excitement, apprehension, pride – these were some of the emotions I experienced that evening. I was eyeballing the spectacle in front of me. Did I really build this thing? Frank interrupted my thoughts:

"Ready?"

"Yep."

"Have you got a fire extinguisher?"

"I'll get one."

"Good. You never know."

I brought the fire extinguisher over and stood it nearby.

"I'm ready Frank."

"Okay!" He turned to Robin waiting in the car. "Kick it in the guts Robin," Frank said with a smile.

I held my breath while Gail fired up her iPad. Robin twisted the ignition key and the engine turned vigorously. But that was all. On the second attempt, it backfired violently twice, before Frank waved frantically to Robin.

"Stop! Something's not right here."

Gail turned her iPad off and Frank began sniffing around under the plenum chamber. I stood by trying hard to hide my disappointment. Presently, Frank disconnected a fuel line and asked Robin to turn the ignition on again. Fuel spurted out and Robin quickly turned it off.

"Plenty of fuel. Plenty of spark. It should go," Frank said looking puzzled.

"Try it again," he told Robin.

Once again the engine turned but would not fire up. Then Frank took some fuel and introduced it directly into the plenum chamber and quickly told Robin to try again. What happened next, took everybody by surprise. An almighty backfire and suddenly the plenum chamber was in flames.

"Fire extinguisher, quick!" Frank shouted, panic stricken.

I was the closest and grabbed the cylinder off the floor, activated it and blasted the side of the engine where the fire was burning. It was only a small extinguisher and I just about exhausted it and not surprisingly, within seconds, it was out. Stunned, the four of us stood rooted to the spot, taking in what had just happened. Frank recovered first.

"How the fuck could that catch alight? It's all sealed!" he declared incredulously, immediately sliding under the car to see where the fire had come from, after flashing me an accusing glance.

The entire left hand side of the engine bay was coated with the contents of the fire extinguisher and by the time poor Frank had emerged from under the car and stood up, so was he. Had it not been such an awkward moment, it would have been funny.

"What are those holes under the plenum chamber?" he asked.

At that very instant I realised what had started the fire. 'Oh my God,' I thought to myself, on the verge of panic. This was another of my famous fuck-ups. Pietersie, you blithering idiot, I screamed inwardly.

"Come over here Frank," I heard myself murmur weakly.

I led him over to a shelf and produced six threaded plugs and dropped them into his palm.

"After the inlet manifold had been cut and shut to miss the bonnet, Peter Mawby looked at it and warned me that there could be welding slag inside the manifold. So the only thing I could think of, was drilling holes opposite the six welds so that I could get something in there to clean them out. I tapped them 16mm and got the plugs to close them up," I confessed, feeling decidedly embarrassed.

"Stick them in," Frank instructed after we cleaned up the mess.

I slid under the car with the six plugs and a spanner and screwed them into place. Once that was done, Frank said to me:

"Shall we try again now Howie?"

This time Robin turned the ignition key and the big engine instantly burst into life and settled down to a lovely even idle – much to my intense relief. It was like listening to beautiful music. I turned to look at Frank. He was standing staring back at me shaking his head, arms folded.

"You had me worried there mate!"

Both Robin and Gail have a somewhat cockeyed sense of humour, and up until the moment the engine started, the two of them had been trying hard to be polite and disguise their amusement. But now, in the aftermath of the fire event, they lost it and began playfully hounding me with great obscenities.

Once that show was over, the four of us attacked a bottle of bubbly that had been quietly waiting on a tray that Gail had brought from the house. We raised our glasses and drank a toast.

Curvy Kate was alive.

The following day John Proud paid me a visit and the subject of a paint job came up.

"Have you met Charlie Gustak?" he enquired.

"No John, but I've seen his place in Oliver Street. Is he the man to talk to?"

"You bet my boy. Old school craftsman. I was with him yesterday. Do yourself a favour Howie and go over there. He's just finished painting an old Rolls. Have a look. I'm sure it will still be there."

"I'll do that," I returned. "It's time to get that ball rolling now."

John, as usual, took more photos of the car and then kept moving as I went back to work. That got me thinking about an all-important subject – for the hundredth time. Colour! At this point the decision was almost made. The petticoat government wanted a burgundy type of shade. I agreed, but with certain reservations. Our Rover is a gorgeous burgundy in bright sunlight, but in overcast weather, she takes on a brown tinge, which is less than pleasing seeing as it took a long time to decide on that colour, which incidentally, was picked from a Hyundai Sante Fe. It was decision time and I didn't want to make the same mistake. Ford had a very smart new colour at the time called 'Seduce'. The day just happened to be overcast and I knew there was a Fairlane in the 'Seduce' colour in the Valley Ford yard. This was my chance to check on it, so I hightailed it over to town to have a look. The car looked just as good as it had in the sunshine. So we decided at last that Curvy Kate would wear the Ford colour, albeit out of step with tradition, as it was a pearl metallic.

My workload was pretty intense at this time, so three days passed before I pulled up outside our local Autopro store to pick up some brake fluid for the Rover. You could flick bottle-tops at Charlie Gustak's place from Autopro, so I just walked over to introduce myself and perhaps initiate something.

His place consisted of an office, one shed full of cars in various stages of restoration and another dedicated to final preparation and painting. The Rolls was still there but Charlie wasn't. A young kid was attacking the rear right fender of an Austin Westminster, with an orbital sander and didn't notice me standing looking at the Rolls. Only the bonnet and part of the right side was visible, as the car was under a cover. One look at the quality assured me on the spot that I was in the right place. Instead of stopping the youngster, I memorised the telephone number which was present on his signboard, and headed back after ringing the number and asking Charlie to reciprocate.

A couple of days later, he was inside my shed carrying out an appraisal of my work, and doing a thorough job of pointing out the many imperfections evident around the car.

"I must fix all these things first," he commented in a guttural central European accent while casting a critical eye on the uneven gap between the front and rear wings.

"That's okay. I realise that. You will find many things to fix," I agreed. "But that's what you guys are for – to fix our fuck-ups. Isn't that true?" I asked him with a smile.

"Oh no," he protested. "Not the fuck-ups – just unfinished. Your job is good. I give you ninety per cent."

"Thank you Charlie. I appreciate ninety per cent."

"How much?" I continued.

"I don't know. Maybe eight thousand, maybe more, maybe less. Maybe we do bit by bit hey?"

"Okay, but if we do it bit by bit, won't it take too long?"

"Maybe two or three months," he offered with some confidence.

I was a little worried about all the 'maybes' but shrugged it off and decided to give him the go ahead.

"Right Charlie, the job is yours," I told him and with that we arranged a date for me to deliver Curvy Kate to his workshop.

Charlie only took around ten weeks longer to finish Curvy Kate than it took Gail to gestate our children.

So, the final analysis goes like this:

I get 90 per cent for construction.

Charlie gets 100 per cent for workmanship and finish.

And Charlie gets 10 per cent for time management.

Hee-hee!

In all seriousness though, Charlie Gustak is, as pointed out by John Proud, a true craftsman, and the exquisite paint job done on Curvy Kate is an absolute credit to him.

CHAPTER TWENTY

EAST EUROPEAN WIZARDRY Over the next five months, there was little to do on Curvy Kate as she was in Charlie Gustak's workshop. Wouldn't it be just my luck that he was constantly interrupted from the long-term jobs by urgent smaller ones. That, among other things, caused Curvy Kate to spend months on 'the back burner'. It made me feel dejected, but I kept up a high profile once I realised what was happening and simply kept chipping away at Charlie. The work progressed steadily as the months dragged by. And then it began to get exciting.

Oh so exciting! Why? Because the telephone rang one day and Charlie Gustak's guttural voice rasped down the line.

"Do you want to come and look?"

"I'm on my way!"

I dropped something important and shot over to Oliver Street at jet speed. This moment had been years in the making and I wasn't going to lose a minute. Inside the booth, a gleaming wonderland of burgundy! Rooted to the spot, I could do nothing but ogle. Charlie had persuaded me to let him purchase a high-quality German brand of paint at a considerably elevated cost. Now I could see why. This was beyond my expectations. It crossed my mind to kiss him on the top of his head like I used to do with Harry, but backed off in case he responded with an East European right hook. So I just shook his hand and rushed off to fetch Gail. I needed to share this with her.

Once the lady entered the booth, she, like myself, ran out of vocabulary. Just a long moment taking in the scene.

"She looks absolutely gorgeous. I think our colour choice was just perfect, don't you?" she beamed.

It was easy to see that this was a decidedly more exciting moment than the time I had broken the news to her about the electronic ignition on our Rover.

Sometime after that day, once Curvy Kate had been brought home and the time consuming job of re-assembly had been concluded, my good friend and motocross buddy, Pat, rang me up. While stuck in a traffic snarl on Albany Highway, he had notice that the car behind him looked "very much like the one you're building". He had got out of his vehicle with the intention of taking some snaps, and struck up a conversation with the two occupants, who turned out to be a couple of boffins from the West Australian Jaguar Club – namely 'JJ' the Club's magazine editor and one Terry McGrath. An exchange of telephone numbers resulted in a visit to Northam by the two men.

Curvy Kate was ultimately embraced by the Jaguar Club despite her dubious pedigree. This, I gathered, would not ruffle any feathers, as the car qualified as a 'special'. So, Gail and I were invited to join the Club which we did and enjoyed some fun times at various Jaguar shows and functions.

In the meantime, the car was finally signed off by the engineer who had happily managed to get Licensing to see sense regarding the reflective chrome saga.

Another memorable moment in the Story of Curvy Kate, was the day the letter arrived from Technical, giving me permission to take her to the pits for inspection.

And in conclusion, I will never forget the wonderful feeling of achievement I experienced on the day she passed her test at Host Autos in Northam.

And now dear reader, my story comes to an end as we take leave of 'Curvy Kate'.

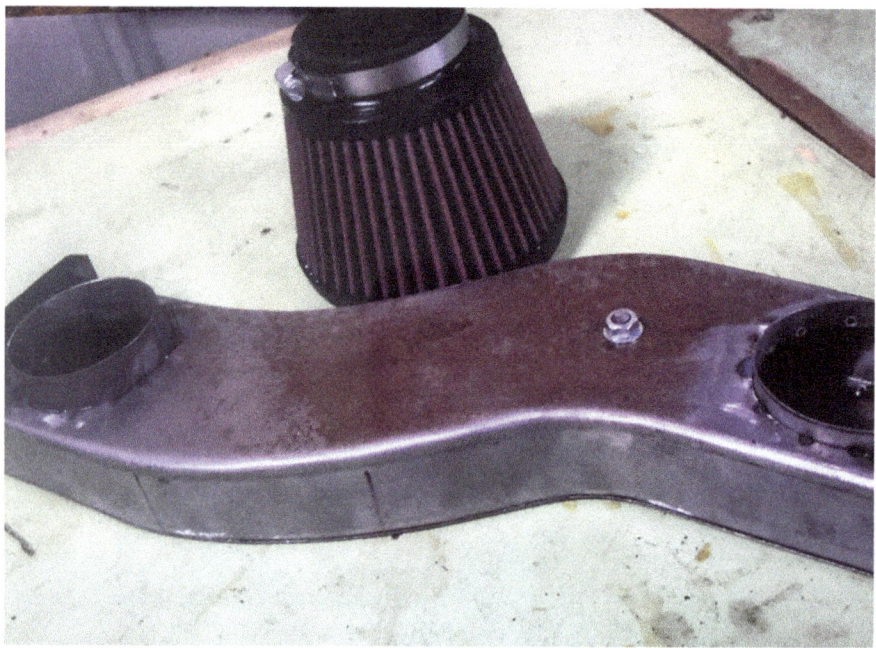

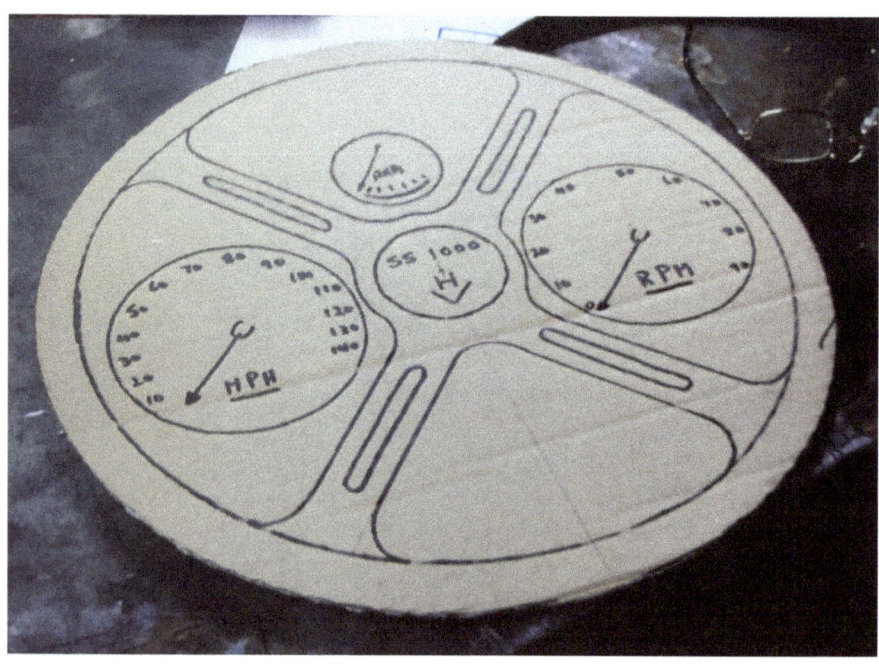

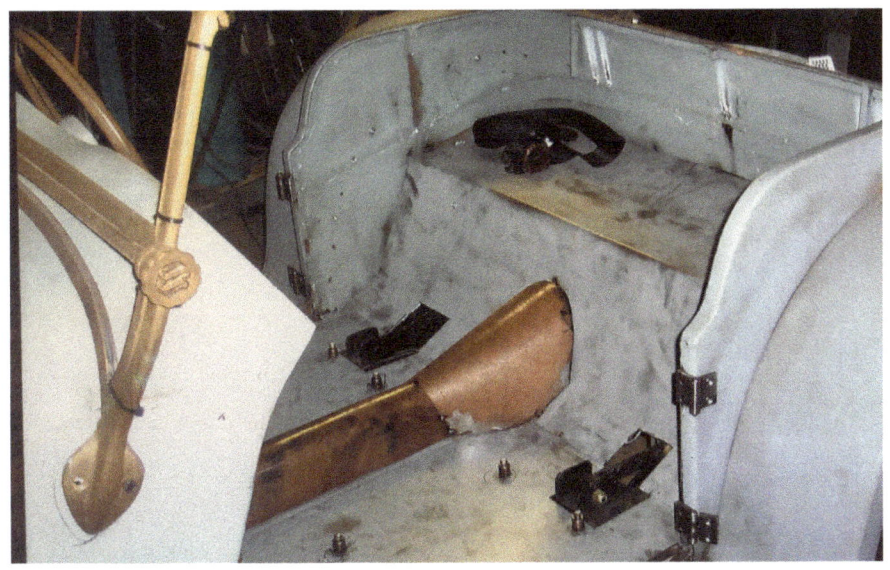

134 | The Story of "Curvy Kate"

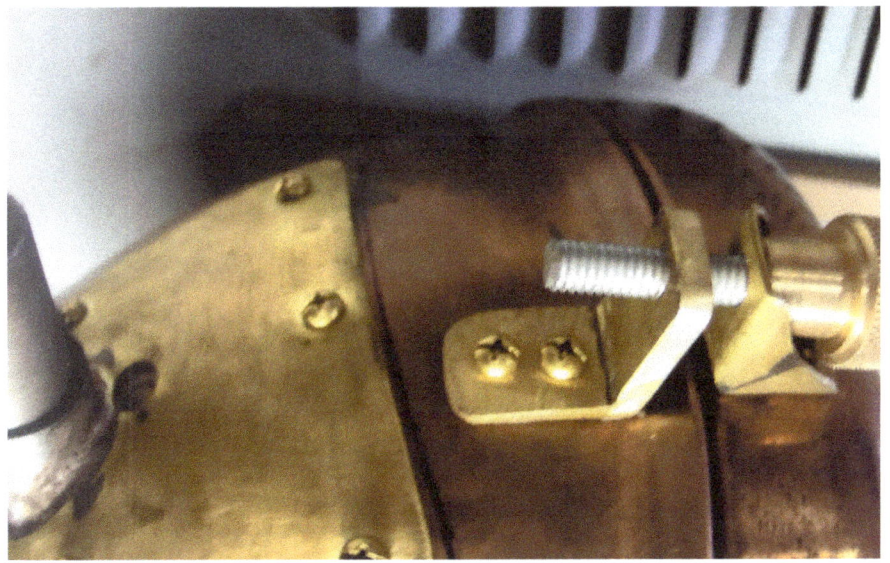

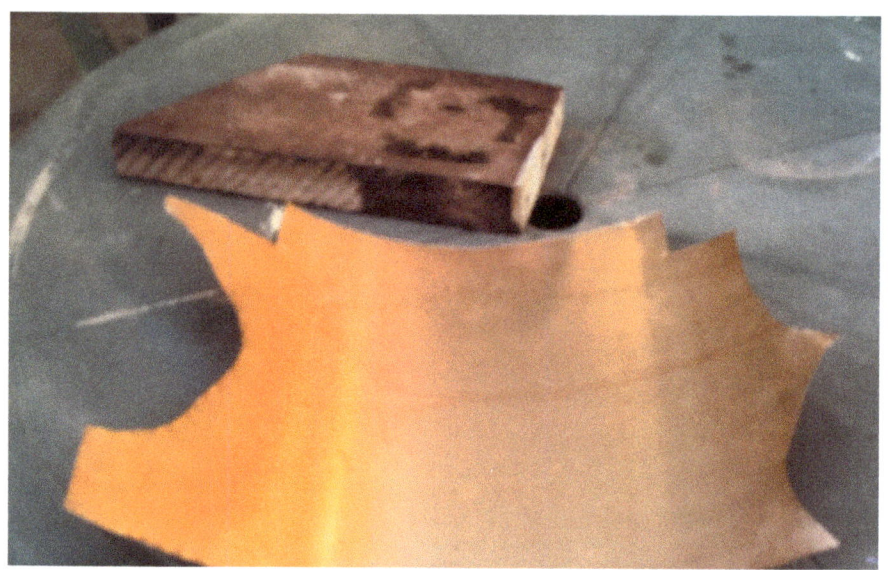

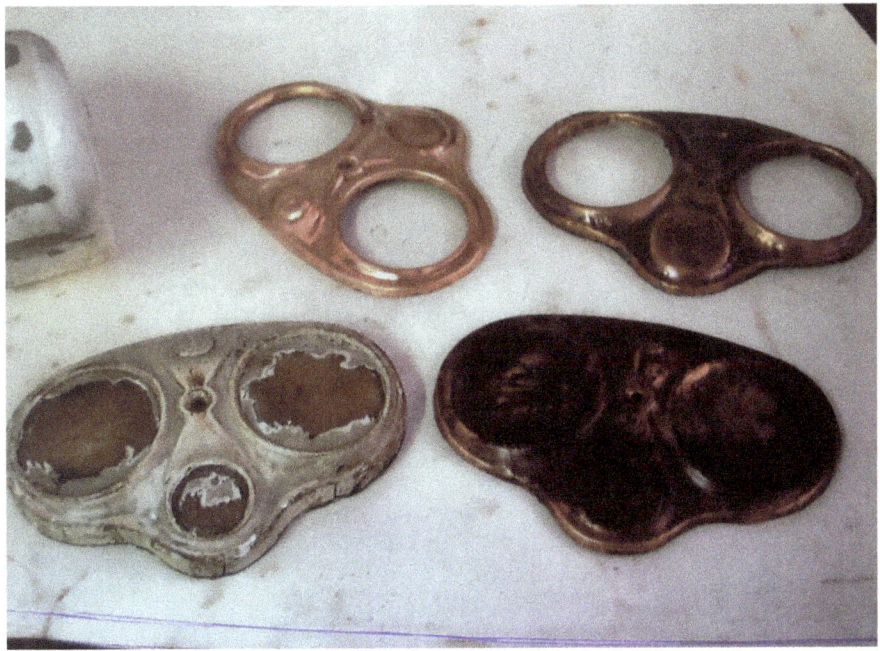

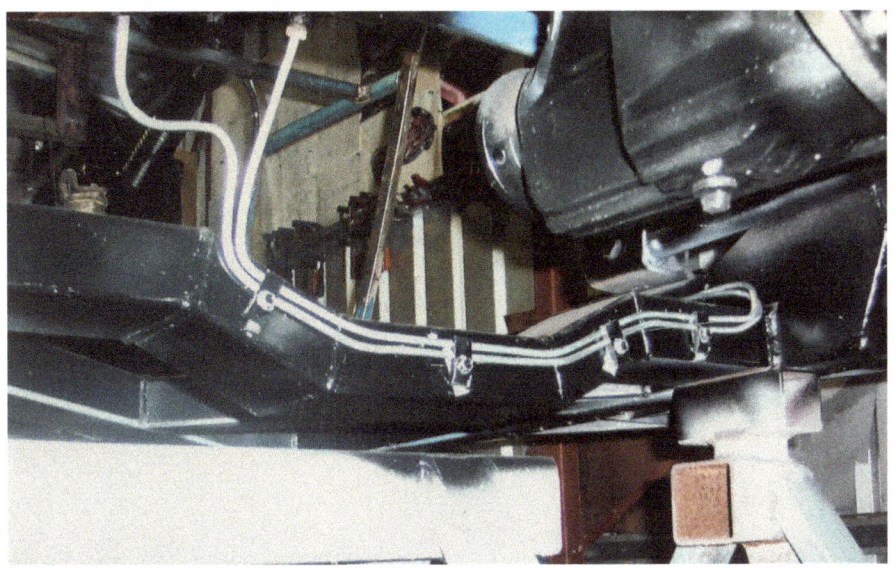

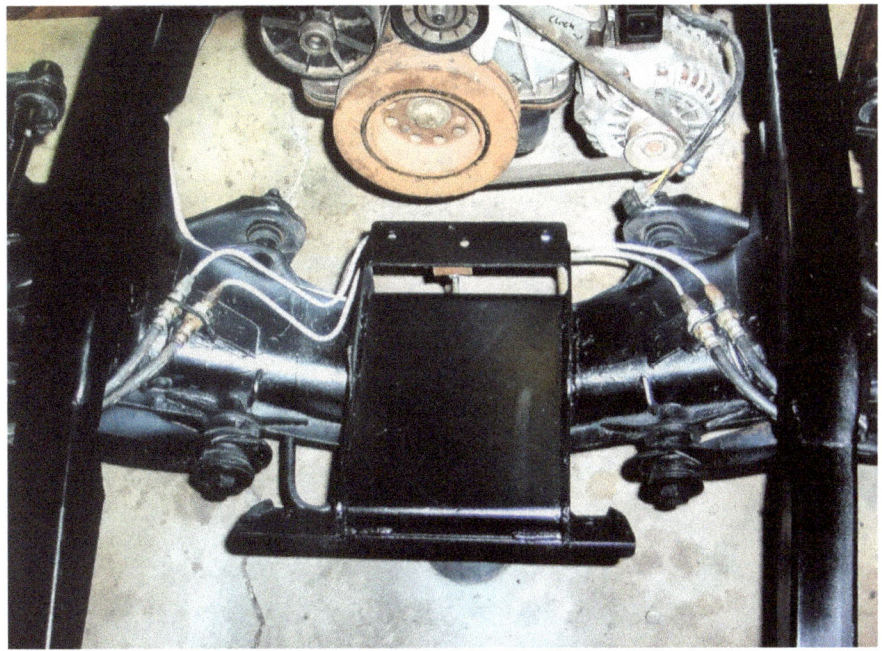

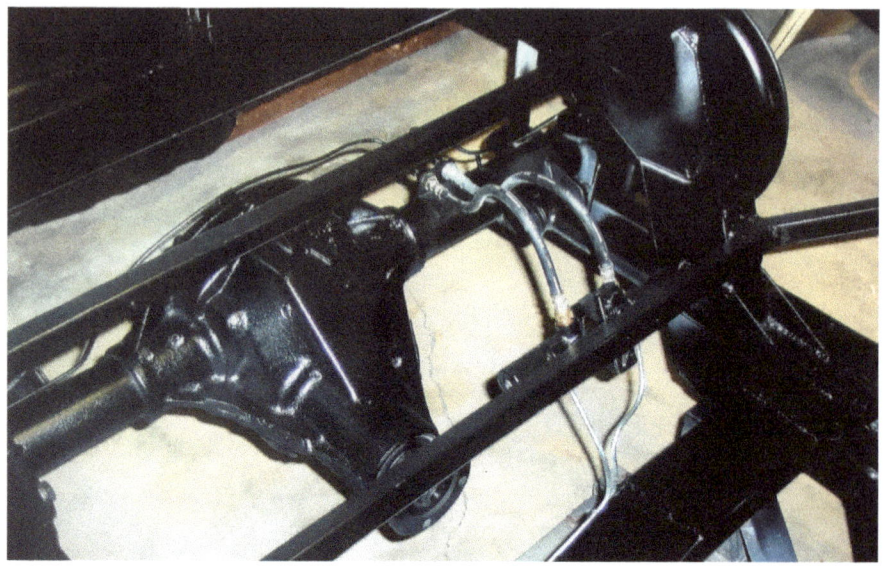

ABOUT THE AUTHOR

The author, Howard James Pietersie, is a South African born Australian citizen, who has lived and worked in Western Australia since emigrating in 1986 at the age of 38 with his wife Gail, son Robin and daughter Anneline.

After serving an apprenticeship, he pursued a career as a marine engineer before meeting the love of his life, Gail Vincent, while on leave in Durban.

After marrying, Gail and Howard lived and worked in various places around South Africa – Gail as a top flight legal secretary and Howard in various engineering positions – until moving to Australia.

The family settled in suburban Perth and ran a successful business, manufacturing display fittings until moving to Northam in the West Australian Wheatbelt where Gail and Howard reside to the present day.

The author has had a passion for British cars for most of his adult life, having owned several Rovers, Minis and Cortinas.

But his greatest ambition was to build a car from 'scratch' so to speak.

The Story of Curvy Kate is the final realisation of that dream.

Howard James Pietersie has also written several short stories and the light-hearted and fast moving fiction adventure novel *Mechanical Mayhem*, which features the larger than life Jack Frost who is a vintage car wheeler dealer, among other things.

The Story of "Curvy Kate"

www.ingramcontent.com/pod-product-compliance
Ingram Content Group UK Ltd.
Pitfield, Milton Keynes, MK11 3LW, UK
UKHW061222180426
11947UKWH00026B/1974